P9-CNH-816

AGNOSTIC

BEYOND

EITHER/OR

MYSTERY

PLAY

LESLEY HAZLETON

RIVERHEAD BOOKS | NEW YORK | 2016

THE SENSE OF AN

ENDING

EVERY

THING

AND MORE

MAKING MEANING

THE THREE-LETTER WORD

AGNOSTIC

A SPIRITED MANIFESTO

IN DOUBT WE TRUST

RIVERHEAD BOOKS
An imprint of Penguin Random House LLC
375 Hudson Street
New York, New York 10014

ISBN 978-1-59463-413-0

Printed in the United States of America
10   9   8   7   6   5   4   3   2   1

BOOK DESIGN BY MARYSARAH QUINN

CONTENTS

ONE

BEYOND
EITHER/OR

THERE ARE SOME FOUR HUNDRED

houseboats in Seattle. Many, like mine, are little more than shacks on rafts, but this may be the only one with a mezuzah at its entrance. If I were religious, the small cylindrical amulet would hold a miniature scroll inscribed with the Shema, the Jewish equivalent of the Lord's Prayer or the Islamic Shahada. But mine doesn't, partly because the scroll kept falling out when I put the mezuzah up on the doorpost, and partly because I don't believe a word of the prayer anyway. I'm not sure what happened to it. I may have thrown it out in a tough-minded moment, or it may be squirreled away at the bottom of a drawer somewhere. No matter. Most of the time I don't even notice the mezuzah, and neither does anyone else. But I know it's there, and that does matter.

Yet why should it? I am firmly agnostic, and haven't

been to a synagogue service in years. Decades, in fact. So is the mezuzah an empty sentimental gesture on my part, or does the word hypocrisy apply? Could I be in denial: a closet theist, or a more deeply closeted atheist? Or am I just a timid fence-sitter, a spineless creature trying to have it both ways, afraid to commit herself one way or the other?

And there's the problem—right there in that phrase "one way or the other." It sees the world in binary terms: yes or no, this side or that. It insists that I can be either agnostic or Jewish but not both, even though both are integral parts of this multi-faceted life that is mine, as integral as being a writer, a psychologist, a feminist, all the many aspects of this particular person I am. All are part of the way I experience the world, and myself in it. Take any one of these aspects away, and I'd be some-one else.

To be agnostic is to love this kind of paradox. Not to skirt it, nor merely to tolerate it, but to actively revel in it. The agnostic stance defies artificial straight lines such as that drawn between belief and unbelief, and shakes off the insistence that it come down on one side or the other. It is free-spirited, thoughtful, and independent-minded—not at all the wishy-washy I-don't-knowness that atheists often accuse it of being. In fact the mocking tone of such accusations reveals the limitations of dogmatic atheism. There's a bullying aspect to it, a kind of schoolyard taunting of agnostics as "lacking the courage of their convictions"—a phrase that raises the question of what exactly conviction has to do with courage. It's easy to forget that the inability to muster the honesty of the three words "I don't know" only leads to a radical dishonesty. The least we have come to expect is that someone be able to bullshit their way out of not knowing something, which is why the first thing taught in media training (a term that always makes me think of obedience training for dogs) is how to evade a difficult question and maintain the tattered illusion of mastery.

I stand tall in my agnosticism, because the essence of it is not merely not-knowing, but something far more challenging and infinitely more intriguing: the magnificent oxymoron inherent in the concept of unknowability. This is the acknowledgment that not everything may be knowable, and that not all questions have definitive answers—certainly not ones as crudely put as the existence or non-existence of God. At its best, however, agnosticism goes further: it takes a spirited delight in not knowing. And this delight is no boorish disdain for knowledge and intellect. Rather, it's a recognition that we need room for mystery, for the imagination, for things sensed but not proven, intuited but not defined—room in which to explore and entertain possibilities instead of heading straight for a safe seat at one end or the other of a falsely created spectrum.

What's been missing is a strong, sophisticated agnosticism that does not simply avoid thinking about the issues, nor sit back with a helpless shrug, but actively explores the paradoxes and possibilities inherent in the vast and varied universe of faith-belief-meaning-mystery-existence. That's my purpose here. I want to explore unanswerable questions with an open mind instead of approaching them with dismissive derision or with the solemn piety of timid steps and bowed head—to get beyond old, worn-out categories and establish an agnostic stance of intellectual and emotional integrity, fully engaged with this strange yet absorbing business of existence in the world.

I HAVE BEEN agnostic for almost as long as I can remember. The only Jew in an English convent school, I
grew up with competing claims on what was presumably
my soul, reciting one grace-before-meals in the convent
and another at home, and wishing I had to do neither.
The school chapel was redolent with the smell of stale
incense, the local Orthodox synagogue with the equally
stale scent of Chanel No. 5 on the fox stole of my mother's neighbor in the women's balcony, where I'd pass the
time by trying to outstare its beady eye. Home offered
the comfort of chopped liver, school the temptation
of pork—and the disappointment when, half-convinced
that the infamous bolt from the blue would strike, I
finally dared take a bite, only to find that it tasted like
boiled chicken. How could something forbidden be so
bland?

Two major religions seemed to be battling for possession of me, making me wonder how it could make any
difference what one stoop-shouldered adolescent believed. Yet while logic seemed to dictate that I would
walk away from all things remotely religious as soon as

I emerged from childhood, that didn't happen. Instead, I compounded my involvement by going to Jerusalem for two weeks and staying for thirteen years. I stayed at first because I was twenty and in love with a classically wrong guy, and then because by the time I'd come to my senses and fallen out of love, I'd already told my university in England to give my research grant to someone else. This was, by any rational measure, a terrible decision, and I have never regretted it.

It was still possible then for a political innocent to romanticize Jerusalem. Mysticism seemed to shimmer in the air. Jewish and Christian and Muslim legends piled on top of one another, laying claim to the same limestone hills and making it easy to imagine that this provincial city had a cosmopolitan soul. I treasured the famous medieval map showing a three-petaled universe with Jerusalem at its hub, and honed my skills in the Center of the World pool hall hidden deep in the alleys of the Old City, not yet aware that thinking of yourself as the center of the world might itself be a sure sign of provincialism. But where the sacred and the profane once seemed to rub shoulders with entrancing ease, they became increasingly indistinguishable. Jerusalem

brought me into the vast and volatile arena in which politics and religion intersect, and as I explored that arena as both a psychologist and a journalist, what I'd thought of as a mysteriously God-haunted city became a city with too much God and not enough humanity.

Three wars later, I moved to Manhattan and then, with the offer of the houseboat, to Seattle. And yet Jerusalem came with me. As the millennium turned, I'd rise every morning to cormorants diving in the mist over Lake Union and sit down at my desk to the deserts of the Middle East, half the world and half of history away. I wrote about Mary in Galilee, Elijah in Gilead, Muhammad in Mecca, and through them, traced the roots of the Big Three monotheisms in the ancient and ongoing search for political and social justice. And I began to blog as an "accidental theologist," describing my posts as "an agnostic eye on religion, politics, and existence," and hoping thus to cover a multitude of sins.

Yet even as I used the word religion, something in me shrank from it, not least because it is so bound up in its origins: the Latin *religari*, to be tied down or constricted. It was no accident that agnostics, unconfined by imposed definitions, were originally called free-thinkers.

Religion seemed an insufficient shorthand for the vast matrix of meaning and experience that it claims to address—a single lens through which to view the multiple facets of what philosopher-psychologist William James called "the varieties of religious experience."

I felt as though I were forging my own exploration of those varieties when I was asked to speak at seemingly unlikely forums for an agnostic: in churches, mosques, and synagogues. "What am I doing here?" I'd think as I stepped in front of the altar. "How on earth did this happen?" Yet people nodded in recognition as I talked about the dismal reduction of mystery to a yes-or-no proposition. They acknowledged a disconnect between what they sensed on the one hand and the demand for belief on the other. Longing for something more than the stark duality of belief/unbelief, they were increasingly impatient with the theist-atheist debate that had produced so much hot air over the previous decade or so. Those involved in that debate seemed increasingly trapped in their own neatly defined binary terms: either/or, true or false. Working with an outdated grab-bag of assertions, they'd reduced complexity to a single dimension, with

the result that the entire issue had become peculiarly overdetermined, in much the same way, say, that New Year's Eve is overdetermined—a single evening too often doomed to disappointment by the sheer weight of expectation vested in it.

I wanted to get beyond the stale tropes of that debate, to rise above its simplistic dichotomies and establish room to breathe, to dance with ideas instead of trying to confine them into conceptual straitjackets. And in this, I was far from alone.

THE MOST RESPECTED POLLS on faith and belief are run by the Pew Forum on Religion and Public Life, which has been taking the pulse of both the American and the international soul, as it were, since 2001. In brief, which is how the Pew results are usually reported, it looks as though we are stuck in a religious time warp. As defined in conventional terms, the United States is apparently as deeply religious a country as when it was founded. Just over two-thirds of Americans say they believe in God. When the question is expanded to "God or a higher power," as in the competing Gallup Poll, that figure rises to 77 percent. And if America seems God-obsessed, Europe appears equally so, with 70 percent of respondents avowing belief.

Nobody seems to ask what is meant by such statements, however. Consider: A stranger calls you on the phone, says she's conducting a survey, and asks if you believe in God. You can answer only yes or no, since don't-knows don't count. And consider too that if you simply hang up, as you're likely to do if you consider this an absurdly simplistic question, you don't count either. So let's assume for the sake of argument that the question intrigues you enough to stay on the line. Yet you may not be quite sure. On the one hand, you don't think of yourself as a believer, not in the usual sense of the word, which defines you as religious. On the other, while you may half-admit this to yourself, saying so out loud to a complete stranger over the phone is something else. Will you be struck by that bolt from the blue if you come out and say no? Is it really any surprise that a certain portion of those still on the line will play it safe and say yes?

There's a similar vagueness when respondents are

asked about their religious affiliation. What exactly does that mean? Am I affiliated or unaffiliated—or do I count twice, once as a Jew and once as an agnostic? I'm not the only one in such an affiliative quandary. It turns out that more than 70 percent of people in England identify as Christian, but since less than 10 percent go to church with any regularity, this apparently means only that they're not Jewish, Muslim, Hindu, Buddhist, or any other readily available religious category. A diminishing few may pop in for a nostalgic Midnight Mass on Christmas Eve, or to light a candle for somebody who's died, but that's about it. Does simply having a Christmas tree define you as Christian, then? Or exclaiming "Jesus!" in exasperation (which would make me a Christian)? Or crossing your fingers in superstitious acknowledgment of the cross on Calvary?

The only thing that seems clear from the polls is that there is a lot of outmoded thinking about religion. Indeed the real question might be if there's any substantial meaning to a term so broad that it covers everything from militant fundamentalism to cultural tradition to an undefined sense of spirituality. Certainly that is the

question asked implicitly by those who stubbornly resist categorization and insist on answering "nothing in
particular" when asked what religion they are.

One in four Americans now rejects the traditional pollster categories, and this group trends young.
More than a third of those under thirty say they are
unaffiliated—a proportion that increases with each new
poll, giving rise to much gray-bearded concern about
millennials losing their way. "Moral compasses" are
often invoked, as though religion always points north. It
doesn't seem to have occurred to the graybeards that
religion and morality are not synonymous—or that ruth-
less minds can turn them into opposites. Nor does it
occur to them that younger people may be deliberately
looking in a different direction, and doing so in such
numbers that they've forced the pollsters to include a
new category, "spiritual but not religious." Close to 40
percent of younger Americans now describe themselves
this way, confounding conservatives hewing to obey-
God's-law legalism.

"Spiritual but not religious" is an expression of a very
human yearning for an opening of mind and heart—
a sense of soul and spirit that enhances day-to-day ex-

perience instead of tamping it down and channeling it into the narrow confines of stick-and-carrot orthodoxy. It's a rejection of traditional tenets and pieties, of doctrine and dogma and judgment. It resists the usual attempts to pigeonhole, saying, "Spare me your labels." It is, at heart, agnostic.

LIKE SO MANY OTHERS, I am tired of stale assumptions—of the demand that I choose sides as though this were some sort of schoolyard game, and of others trying to convince me. In fact I am tired of conviction, and of the preaching and scolding of those who claim a comfortable perch from which to preen their righteous feathers, whether religious or irreligious. Conviction is not only to be convinced; it's also to be convicted, like a prisoner in his cell. It is to close one's mind, to nail oneself down beyond a shadow of doubt—a turn of phrase that sees doubt as a threat, some darkness lurking in your peripheral vision like an intruder to be vanquished instead of as a partner to curiosity and a prerequisite to real thought.

I see no reason to accept the terms of those who would consign me to some kind of intellectual or spiritual no-man's-land (or in my case, presumably, no-woman's-land). For years, their books piled up on my floor, a verbal minefield of impassioned arguments mistaking conviction for evidence, intensity for fact—so many books that they weighed down the houseboat, making it ride low in the water. Not for nothing are tomes called weighty. The nether reaches of philosophy and theology are thickets of near-impenetrable prose, but I persisted nonetheless, only to deepen the feeling that I was witnessing the most sophisticated minds perform extraordinary contortions in order to answer questions that by definition have no answer.

I found myself grumbling like crazy in the margins of these books—railing at assertions presented as axiomatic, at the piling up of things-taken-for-granted, at received wisdom presented as fact. Penciled question marks proliferated, often turning into scrawled No's of exasperation and then into scribbled rebuttals along the tops or the bottoms of the pages. I was arguing with saints and sages, holding running conversations with men dead for centuries as though they could talk back to me.

The "new atheists"—I rattle off the most prominent with the mnemonic H_2D_2 (Harris, Hitchens, Dawkins, and Dennett)—were certainly more readable, favoring polemic over philosophy. But their contemptuous tone made it clear that even the most determined rationalists can lose their balance and allow wittily phrased generalizations to stand in for clarity of thought. Like Christopher Hitchens, one can certainly point to all the horrors committed in the name of religion—God knows there's a long blood-soaked history of them. But to then argue as he did that religion itself is evil is deeply illogical. You could as well point to all the horrors committed in the name of love, and then claim that love itself is evil.

I thought of these lines from the W. B. Yeats poem "The Second Coming": "The best lack all conviction, while the worst / Are full of passionate intensity." Yet both conviction and passionate intensity were on rampant display on my floor, from men—and they were indeed nearly all men—who quite evidently considered themselves the best. Far from lacking, conviction was actually the source of their passionate intensity, so much so that another phrase came to mind: Jean-Paul Sartre's existential *mauvaise foi*, the inauthenticity of bad faith.

There came the day when I could no longer stand threading my way through these piles of tomes. I collected cardboard boxes and made a couple of runs to the storage locker. My house rose again in the water, and I sat down to write, similarly unburdened. It was time to bring my argument out of the margins and into the center of the page. Time to expand the whole debate—to raise it up off the floor and perhaps achieve a kind of *dis*-passionate intensity. Time, that is, to get beyond either/or, yes-or-no answers, because while such a digital way of thinking may be excellent for computers, it is downright dangerous for human beings. The grim joylessness of fundamentalism is testament to that.

I wanted to bring color to the table—to explore the richly textured existential terrain in which we really live instead of the narrow black-and-white one in which preachers and pundits have tried to confine us. And I believe most of us are ready for such an exploration. Some may identify as religious, despite their doubts; some as agnostic, even if not quite sure what they mean by this; some as atheist, if with occasional misgivings and fingers crossed behind their backs. But most, I think, will agree that we don't all have to be on exactly the same page, that we have nothing to lose but the false consolation of forced labels, and that it's way past time to approach this whole complex, often crazed subject of faith-belief-meaning-mystery-existence not as something to be "solved," but as an ongoing, open-ended adventure of the mind.

Think of this book, then, as an exploration of the agnostic perspective, of the zones of thought that open up once you break free of deceptively neat categorizations, and that then feed back into each other in fresh and unexpected ways. Each of the following chapters focuses on one such zone. I start by challenging the attempt to corral the sense of what we call the divine and cut it down to human size. From there, I confront the misleading conflation of belief with faith. Looking squarely at how we have idolized certainty and demonized doubt, I highlight the creative value of doubt, without which real faith is impossible. Instead of insisting on a "theory of everything," I consider the vital role of mystery in a deceptively information-rich world; ask what we mean by the search for meaning; question the assumption that we all necessarily fear death and yearn for the cold realm of immortality; and unpack the heady concept of infinity, the humbling yet elating perspective of infinite time and space. And finally, I explore the "we" involved here—the elusive but undeniable phenomenon of consciousness, of the human mind thinking about the fact that it can think at all—and argue with spirit for a sense of soul, free of such qualifiers as "blessed" and "immortal."

Throughout, what impels me is a desire to rise above the plethora of things-taken-for-granted, to shrug off the multiple tyrannies of the definite article (*the* truth, *the* soul, *the* universe, *the* meaning of life), and to find more honest ways—both intellectually and emotionally—to talk about such magnificent intangibles as God, infinity, and consciousness.

To those looking for certainty, such a stance will be nothing short of a nightmare. It embraces both possibility and its correlate, uncertainty. It suspects all absolutes, all simplifications. It refuses the balkanization of thought and steps over the territorial lines between philosophy, psychology, theology, physics, and metaphysics. Instead of either/or, it thinks more in terms of "and"—reason *and* imagination, logic *and* intuition. It takes delight in the play of ideas, and resists all attempts to channel and shoehorn them into the narrow constraints of conviction.

No "answers" here, then. I make no claim to truth,

let alone "the Truth," buttressed with that capital letter to give it a kind of unassailable grandeur. There are already far too many people convinced that they are the possessors of such presumptuous truth, and I do not intend to add to their number. Neither do I have any desire to preach, or to convert anyone to agnosticism. In fact I'd take the "ism" out of that word if I could, since the last thing needed is yet another pompously "complete" system of thought and belief demanding adherence to some sort of party line.

So while I offer this book as an agnostic manifesto, I recognize that it's a strange kind of manifesto indeed—one that makes no claims to truth, offers no certainties, eschews brashly confident answers to grand existential questions. And if this makes it a peculiarly paradoxical creature, that is exactly what it needs to be, because to be agnostic is to cherish both paradox and conundrum. It is to acknowledge the unknowable and yet explore it at the same time, and to do so with zest, in a celebration not only of the life of the mind, but of life itself.

TWO

THE THREE-LETTER
WORD

GOD IS SUCH A LITTLE WORD FOR

such a huge concept. A mere three letters in English, it's so short, so concise, so . . . familiar. Far more user-friendly than the amorphous idea of the divine or the transcendent or the infinite, it's really a kind of nickname, a shorthand claim to intimacy. The insistent uppercase G helps make it personal. It asserts existence, as though this were something, even someone, you could wrap not just your head but your arms around, which may be why people talk of embracing God or religion. In effect, the three-letter word brings a grand concept down to size. Human size, that is.

Naming God invites the personal pronoun—He, Him, His, all capitalized like the name itself, and all with a kind of male inevitability. Monotheism's male gendering of divinity has run so deep for so long that you only need to refer to God as "she" for people to be taken aback. Try using "it," and most will react with visible shock; even militant atheists will respond with a quiver of transgressive thrill.

But what exactly is being transgressed? The uncanny otherness of "it" seems to me to accord much greater respect than either "he" or "she," though even it has its drawbacks. It still assumes an entity—something that can be described, defined, apprehended, encompassed. By even asking whether God "really exists," all we bring about is an extraordinary diminution of the concept of the divine, so much so that for a growing number of people, the name has become little more than a convention, even an almost embarrassing one, like an outmoded term of endearment. Trying to make the unknowable knowable, we reduce it to what we know best. We make God human.

God is not the only victim of this propensity. Perhaps because we're social animals and thus crave company, we tend to humanize as many things as we can. We see ourselves reflected in household pets, cars, clouds, the moon, even something you'd think as defiantly inhuman as stone. Friends who'd occasionally join me in the course of the year I spent wandering the Sinai Desert would delight in picking out human and animal shapes in rock formations, seeing them as reassuringly familiar presences in a landscape they experienced as threateningly empty. I kept wishing they wouldn't.

"But you're not seeing the rock itself," I'd protest. A newly minted desert purist, I knew just enough geology to be awed at the fact that this was where hundreds of millions, even billions, of years were laid out before your eyes. Stone, the most immovable thing imaginable— stony-hearted, stone-cold, dead as a stone—was revealed as hot, malleable, even fluid. You could read time in the striations of naked rock that had been contorted, thrust up, bent, folded, arched, and swirled by tectonic and volcanic forces. This was not mere human time, but geological time, in which *Homo sapiens* has existed for less than an eyeblink. I'd find nautilus fossils laid down when this whole desert was an ocean bed; lose my balance as I tried to conceive of the entire landscape in flux; shiver in the heat with the awareness of the primordial.

Even as those millions and billions of years tripped off my tongue, however, I was aware that neither my friends nor I had any idea what these numbers actually meant. We can conceive of such time, but only abstractly. It's beyond human grasp—truly inhuman. What struck me above all, then, was the ineffable otherness of the desert, and it was this otherness that awed me. I had no desire to make it less "other" by finding familiar shapes and thus imposing my own terms of reference. Yet once those shapes had been pointed out, I couldn't help seeing them too.

As storytellers have always known and psychologists have only recently confirmed, humans are pattern-seeking creatures. That is, we seek out narrative. Or rather, we impose it. This is the dynamic behind the stories we tell of ourselves, editing and curating them so that they "make sense." We search for a through thread: a linear narrative instead of a series of more or less random occasions where, consciously or not, we went this way instead of that. We discover intention, or perhaps invent it. Thus the unnerving ease of the "elevator résumé," a whole life compressed into the time it takes to travel a few floors in an elevator, or the popularity of memoirs, in which messy realities have been edited out. We create meaning, and in so doing, obey the narrative need for a protagonist.

The monotheistic creator god that arose out of the stark stone deserts of the Middle East is perhaps the grandest protagonist ever created. This god of tectonic and volcanic forces was as far removed as possible from the god of the personal pronoun, yet that use of "he" would close the gap between human and divine. It seemed inevitable that he would have a hand (always just one, for some reason). He'd have eyes and ears and a voice. Lungs ("the breath of God upon the waters") and even feet ("He shall tread down our enemies," sang the psalmist). And along with such physical characteristics, he would develop a mind, a will, and a personality as contradictory as any human's. Rendered equally capable of anger and love, vengeance and generosity, jealousy and forgiveness, he became not merely capricious, but intolerant.

When Adam and Eve are banished from Eden in the third chapter of Genesis, God is depicted as a punitive tyrant intent on absolute control of his creations. Their desire for the fruit of the tree of knowledge seems to me both necessary and praiseworthy, but to the biblical author it was a crime against authority. And while he may have intended the expulsion from Eden as a message of divine power, the history of religion is rife with unintended consequences. What resulted was an extraordinarily petty, misogynistic idea of the divine, an easy target for Enlightenment philosophers like Montesquieu, who quipped that "were triangles to invent a god, they would give him three sides." Voltaire took a similar tack, tartly noting that "while God may have made us in his image, we have paid him back in kind." No modern atheist has put it better. The anthropomorphic idea of God says far more about humans than about anything remotely transcendent.

AN OLD WOMAN draped in shawls used to sit on the pavement across from the post office on Jerusalem's Jaffa Road, selling amulets. People bought the tightly scrolled pieces of paper bound in colored twine partly for good luck, but mainly as a means of charity without condescension. Most never gave the amulets more than a passing thought, but when she assured a poet friend that his contained God's phone number, he opened it up to find a local number written inside. He called it several times, but nobody answered. When he saw her next and told her this, she smiled sweetly and said, "Isn't that just like God? Never there when you're looking for him."

Yet despite this wry piece of folk wisdom, people keep trying. Go into any small church in Latin America or the Middle East, and you'll find votives. Not just candles, but clay or metal models of arms, legs, hearts, livers, all manner of body parts, hung alongside or behind the altar. Often there are notes attached to them, prayers for healing that particular limb or organ in a loved one, or letters beginning "Dear Jesus," in the kind of painstaking writing you know has been copied out many times until it came out right. Sometimes, heartbreakingly, there are photographs too—of a horribly sick child, for instance, as though the sight of the bald head and the plastic tubing will finally make God take pity.

Orthodox Jews do much the same, placing written prayers and pleas between the huge ashlar stones of the Western Wall. Throughout the Middle East and North Africa, Muslims decorate shrines of sages and folk saints with ribbons and amulets, while in Japan, the trees of Shinto shrines are hung with paper prayer strips. Such practices are expressions of a very human longing for a palpable connection to the divine. Even as the pious talk derisively of pre-Christian "godless pagans" (an oxymoron, since these were actually polytheists, living in a world full of gods rather than one with none at all), they continue the traditions of those they so despise. First fruits, garlands, votives, letters, flowers, promises, coins, tithes, offerings both burned and raw: all reveal the desire for a divinity that "exists" in human terms, something that can be seen, touched, spoken to, implored. Some "thing," that is—some *one*—with which to have a relationship, even physical intimacy as in kissing the crucifix, the ground, the black stone, the wall.

Inevitable, perhaps. Since few of us are mathematicians, we're not very good at dealing with abstractions. We need to concretize. We need metaphors—the kind of striking images that fix things in our mind's eye (a metaphor right there). Even the most literal fundamentalist will acknowledge that the hand, voice, and eyes of God are metaphorical, but that doesn't mean they're "merely" symbolic. In the influential coinage of cognitive linguist George Lakoff, they're metaphors we live by. "Our ordinary conceptual system," he wrote, "is fundamentally metaphorical in nature."

Metaphors aren't just for poets. Or perhaps we're all poets without knowing it, because metaphors are built into the way we think. We use them almost automatically. They work their way deep into our minds, mediating and shaping how we see the world, how we understand ourselves in it, even how we interact with it. The metaphor that gave rise to the word religion, for instance—*religari*, to be bound—is acted out in rituals such as the sevenfold circling of the black-draped Kaaba during the hajj pilgrimage in Mecca. Left shoulders in— the side where the heart is—pilgrims bind themselves with their bodies to the place and everything it stands for. Hindu pilgrims do the same at shrines of holy figures, as does the bride in a traditional Jewish wedding ceremony when she circles the groom seven times.

One of the strongest religious metaphors is that of height. God is thus "the highest," or at least a "higher power." When evangelical Christians raise eyes and arms skyward as they pray, they take their cue from the worship of the ancient sky god (Baal, Zeus, or Yahweh, depending on where you lived), shown in statuettes wielding a lightning bolt. Their practice happens to be a clear negation of the monotheistic principle of God as universal or omnipresent, and thus surely as real and present at your feet as in the clouds. But metaphor trumps principle.

We have a long history of altars built on high places, presumably on the basis of "nearer my God to thee," whatever god or gods might be involved. The heavenly counterpart is hell, stoked by fires of molten lava deep beneath the earth's surface—the hadopelagic, from Hades, the deepest depths. And this meme of heaven above and hell below suffuses everyday speech, making it easy to assume that what's high is good, "above reproach," while what's low is bad, "the bottom of the heap" or "beneath contempt." The human race has been seen as the pinnacle of evolution, and humans as a higher order of creation. Some are even called high-functioning. We have upper and lower classes, both socioeconomic and biological, and upper and lower cases, as in the name God. We have high and low IQ, high and low times, high and low achievement, hi-def, hi-fi, hi-res. Our spirits can sink or soar. We get high and feel low. And above all, as it were, we occasionally engage in high-level negotiations, rise above our emotions, and give each other a resounding high-five.

Michelangelo may have had no choice but to paint

God on the ceiling of the Sistine Chapel instead of on the wall. And while few people are under the illusion that the bearded old man "up there" is anything other than a visual metaphor, no matter how good his musculature, it makes sense nonetheless that even as he stretches out his arm, he should be beyond reach, forcing mere mortals to look up, straining necks and eyes for a glimpse of what's often called "something larger."

You might intuit this something larger, even catch a glimpse of it as though out of that corner of your mind's eye. On a mountaintop at sunset, for instance, or when listening to music. Or in meditation or prayer, or on a psychedelic drug, or in the most common "oh God" moment of all, which is orgasm. Any of these and more are moments of what Freud called "oceanic consciousness," of being lifted out of your separate self into a feeling of being without boundaries, part of some greater whole. Whether you call such moments intimations of the divine or, more mundanely, altered states of consciousness, you recognize them as going beyond your everyday existence and thus think of them as metaphysical—literally, beyond physics. Beyond comprehension, that is. In the realm of mystery.

Try to talk about mystery, though, and you are stuck with words and images that seem to circle around the experience without ever touching it, because despite all the attempts of mystics great and small, real and not-so-real, mystery is inexpressible. That's the essence of it. It's as though we're left with no option but to fall back on the familiar three-letter word, however corrupted it has been by literalism and anthropomorphism, and even as we sense that it's oddly inadequate.

A SMALL GLASS VIAL occupies pride of place in a showcase at the Henry Ford Museum in Dearborn, Michigan. I thought it was a mistake at first—something left behind by a careless curator—since the vial, really just a rubber-stoppered test tube, is empty. Then I noticed the label beside it: "Thomas Edison's last breath."

That kind of took my breath away. I stood there mesmerized, half-amused and half-revolted as I imagined Ford hovering over Edison's deathbed waiting for the last breath. But how would he have known which was the last one until it was too late? And why did the last breath have such significance for him? Did he know that the same word is used for breath and spirit in Hebrew (*nefesh*) and Arabic (*nafas*)? Since he was a notorious anti-Semite, I was pretty sure not. Or did he think he'd caught the soul of his idol, Edison, at the moment he believed it had left the body? I had a horrible idea he did. In which case, it was hard to imagine a worse metaphor for the soul than an empty test tube.

Far better men than Ford have spent inordinate amounts of ink and energy trying to pin down not just the soul but the much larger concept of God, as though they could definitively prove the existence or non-existence of something that is by definition beyond definition. Indeed, much of theology can be seen as an endless gnawing at this particular metaphysical bone, starting with the Bible itself. "Truly you are a God who hides yourself," says Isaiah, while the psalmist laments divine silence in the face of suffering: "My God, my God, why have you forsaken me?"—the words quoted by Jesus in the agony of crucifixion. "I cry, but you do not answer."

No matter how many theologists have felt compelled to devise what they saw as rational proofs of the existence of God, their work still feels haunted by absence. As W. H. Auden wryly reflected, such "proofs or disproofs that we tender" bounce back "unopened to the sender." In fact the cumulative number of such proofs over the centuries is itself suspect, since it should go without saying that if any one were workable, all the others would not be necessary—a point made with wit and elegance in philosopher Rebecca Goldstein's novel *36 Arguments for the Existence of God* (subtitled *A Work of Fiction*), in which each argument is carefully presented and equally carefully picked apart.

Perhaps the most famous attempt to rationalize belief is known as Pascal's wager. In a quick couple of pages in his *Pensées*, the seventeenth-century mathematician-turned-theologist took a deadpan poke at the whole question of the existence of God by reducing it to the terms of a simple coin toss: heads, God exists; tails, God does not exist. Impossible to get more either/or than that. And while you might think that the only sensible response would be to refuse the wager as absurdly reductive, Pascal wouldn't allow that out. Logicians are very good at establishing their own rules for the games they play, and he insisted that for some unstated reason, you must bet one way or the other—no ums, ahs, ifs, buts, or maybes allowed.

"Let us weigh up the gain and the loss in calling heads that God exists," he said. On the one hand, if you bet heads and you are right, your gain is "an eternity of life and happiness" in heaven. Moreover, there is practically no penalty if you are wrong. True, you will presumably have forgone what he called the "noxious pleasures" attributed to nonbelievers—no booze, no sex outside marriage, no unbridled greed—but to an ascetic like Pascal, such a sacrifice was negligible. On the other hand, if you bet against God, you may gain the freedom to indulge in whatever noxious pleasures you can conceive of, thinking yourself free of any blowback in an afterlife you don't believe exists. But if you are wrong— and since it's a coin toss, the odds are fifty-fifty that you are—what you get is eternal damnation.

Et voilà! Infinity is in the balance: eternal reward versus eternal punishment. That being so, Pascal concluded, the only rational option is to bet in favor of God. "If you win, you win all," he announced. "If you lose, you lose nothing. Wager, then, without hesitation, that God is."

Put this way, it sounds quite irresistible: the kind of offer you'd be on the alert for in incoming spam, or something you'd expect from a tout at the racetrack or a scam artist in Times Square. As Pascal was well aware, the wager is stacked, not least because it assumes a rigid, authoritarian deity meting out punishment as ruthlessly as the most repressive military regime. Essentially, he was making an insurance salesman's argument. The salesman asks you for an impossible assessment: How long are you going to live? Err on the side of caution and assume a long life, and you will start writing hefty checks. Err the other way and assume a short life, and you may leave your family destitute. Even as you pay your premiums, you suspect that you're being taken for a ride, but you don't dare not pay, since you can't be certain. The same logic applies as in the infamous wager: heaven or hell in religious terms, financial solvency or insolvency in earthly ones. Pascal's argument for belief was thus a form of life insurance. Or rather, afterlife insurance.

Yet by presenting belief in God not as a matter of faith but as a decision-making problem—a choice, even if only a binary one—Pascal turns out to be startlingly modern. It was only in the twentieth century that religion really became a matter of choice for all but a small intellectual elite, at least in the West. For most of his-

tory, there was no widespread distinction between religious and secular, nor of religion as a specific category of thought and belief. Nor was belief required, because religion was self-evident: it explained everything, from drought and flood to life and death. What is theology, after all, but an older version of the scientific quest for a unified theory, the elusive "theory of everything"? Theology provided a cogent narrative of existence, and most people found comfort in that. Except, it seems, for theologists themselves.

A FRIEND ONCE devised the most extraordinarily elegant proof that minus two times minus two equals plus four. The question had obsessed me for a while, all the more since most mathematicians I'd asked had replied with some version of "That's just the way it is." I could even be seen trying to pace it out on the street, muttering to myself as I went two steps by two backward and forward, so this proof—just five short lines—came as a relief. I copied it down and kept it tucked in my wallet, and because I had it on paper, saw no need to memorize it. I wish I had. The wallet was stolen a few years later,

and by then the friend who'd come up with those five lines had died. I've since asked any number of mathematicians if they can reproduce it, and though a few have produced longer proofs, none was as perfect as that one remains in my memory, hovering beyond reach.

It was a negative proof, as the most elegant ones often are. That is, instead of proving the answer directly, it proved that any other answer was impossible. Over the centuries, many theologists have adopted a similar approach. With varying degrees of elegance, they have tried to define God not by specific human attributes, but precisely by the lack of them. This is known as negative or "apophatic" theology—a word I note in fascination at the tendency to head straight for the most abstruse terms possible.

An early example comes courtesy of one of the last people I would ever have thought to find myself citing in this respect: Saint Paul. In the Acts of the Apostles, which is basically a progress report on the growth of the early Christian church, he mentions passing by a Greek temple dedicated to the *agnostos theos*, the unknown god. It turns out that he mentions it only in order to tear it

down, at least with words. But I remain grateful to him nonetheless for the image, because while he was horrified at what he saw as flagrant ignorance, such a temple seems to me an immensely moving idea. It brings to mind the Tomb of the Unknown Soldier, or the rough white crosses at the heads of so many unidentified World War I battlefield graves, whole fields of them haunted by the presence of absence.

Since Paul, however, sophisticated theologists have consistently argued for the unknown god. Or rather, the unknown capitalized God. And herein lies the problem. Even as they try to get beyond anthropomorphism, they find themselves trapped in it, talking of God as He and Him and thus tying themselves in conceptual knots (an occupational hazard of philosophy in general, but especially so in the philosophy of religion). In effect, they become prisoners of an intellectual double bind. They conceive of God as transcendent and thus beyond human grasp, but are then left grasping for a language in which to describe something for which no language exists. Trying to define God by what he is not rather than what he is, they still hew to that personal pronoun and thus run the risk of losing their own argument in the same breath they make it.

Despite himself, for example, Saint Thomas Aquinas wrote of God as a "being" with a self and a will, and contradicted his own argument of unknowability by falling back on the personal pronoun ("to love God is greater than to know Him"). Maimonides, the great medieval codifier of Jewish law and ethics whose *Guide for the Perplexed* still acts as just that, wrote persuasively that God is beyond human knowledge, yet at every mention of the name, he added, "May He be exalted." Pascal resorted to the language of gambling because "if there is a God, He is infinitely beyond our comprehension . . . He bears no relation to us; we are therefore incapable of knowing either what He is or whether He is." Even Spinoza, the ecstatic rationalist who spurned anthropomorphic concepts as superstitious folklore and instead devoted his life to building a logical framework for understanding God, couldn't avoid the pronoun ("God acts and guides all things only from the necessity of His own nature and perfection"). But perhaps the most startling apophatic formulation came from the lesser-known Irish-born scholar John Scotus Erigena, who perfectly encapsulated the dilemma back in the ninth century. "We do not know what God is," he wrote. "God Himself does not know what He is because He is not anything. Literally, God is not, because He transcends being."

This is the problem with trying to describe the ineffable. By definition, something that's ineffable is beyond words, so the use of words appears doomed to failure. Any attempt to pin down the intangible finds itself ensnared in the all-too-tangible. And this irony is only compounded when you realize that atheists seem to share in the popular desire for a tangible god.

Freud, that founding analyst of personal relationships, was one of the first. He mocked those he accused of "giving the name of 'God' to some vague abstraction which they have created for themselves." Such philosophers, he continued, "boast that they have recognized a higher, purer concept of God, notwithstanding that their God is now nothing more than an insubstantial shadow and no longer the mighty personality of religious doctrines. Critics persist in describing as 'deeply religious' anyone who admits to a sense of man's insignificance or impotence in the face of the universe, although what constitutes the essence of the religious attitude is not this feeling but only the next step after it, the reaction to it which seeks a remedy for it."

That "mighty personality" was apparently exactly what Freud wanted—a good old-fashioned god who could take action, wield a lightning bolt or two on demand, and thus prove himself anything but insubstantial. A god, presumably, who could be analyzed. Yet by sneering at abstraction and insisting on remedies, Freud assumed as deeply as someone praying for a miracle that God should be functional. And in this he set the tone for modern atheists who scoff at talk of a mysterious, transcendent god. "What's the use of a god like that?" they ask. Victims of the utilitarian fallacy, they demand that God be practical—some kind of divine mobile app or problem-solver, or at least someone who'll answer the phone. Even as they reject the depressingly dour idea of God as a taskmaster meting out reward and punishment, they seem to hanker for something very close to it. Insisting that there has to be some purpose in "having" a god even as they deny there is one, they place themselves in the same flat dimension as those believers who condescendingly pity the purpose-less beings they see as lacking one.

YOU ALMOST HAVE to admire the presumptuous absurdity of the word godless. It posits God as a thing to be owned (the expression "my God" comes to mind, or the twittery "OMG")—a possession that can be sought out and acquired, or cast aside once you've grown tired of it or discovered that it doesn't work as advertised. As with your keys or your wallet, you "find" God or "lose" your faith. Whether you believe or don't believe, you're stuck in a vast lost-and-found department, presumably of the soul.

The assumption behind such language is that the believers are in possession of something that others lack. They are the spiritual haves, while the godless are the have-nots, or in the preferred pious parlance, "lost souls." The language of superiority is unmistakable. But this is more than a mere preening of righteous religious feathers; it's an assumption of strength, which depends on the idea that to be lost is a sign of weakness. It is, in short, an accusation.

To lose one's way, whether on the road or in life, is to be rendered open to the unknown, with none of the usual safeguards of familiarity. It is to be vulnerable. Perhaps that's why few of us, atheists included, can hear the hymn "Amazing Grace" and remain unmoved by it. "I once was lost and now am found" expresses a painful, almost childlike yearning for comfort from the terrors of the night or of a dark forest, the sense of a long and perilous road traveled. Though originally written by an English cleric, it has become the American anthem of hard times endured. Sung best in a lone voice without musical accompaniment, it is a hymn of fragility, and it's precisely this fragility that makes it so powerful. There is no sense of triumph or self-congratulation. The singer is not proud; she takes no credit for having found her way, and every lonesome note sounds the awareness of how tenuous this sense of direction can be. But what strikes me most about the hymn is the absence of judgment. It doesn't see vulnerability as weakness, because it has no need to do that. It accepts being lost as part of being human, and sees no shame in it. And in this, it remains an outlier.

Those who are most terrified of being lost tend to

be those who are the most judgmental about it. The genuine humility of "Amazing Grace" evades them; indeed the louder they proclaim their humility, the clearer their lack of it becomes. They see religion not as acceptance of vulnerability but as a means of warding it off—a kind of divine insurance against losing their way.

Yet what is so very wrong about losing one's way? I can see that there's a certain security in being solidly positioned between point A and point B on a kind of existential GPS screen, though it seems to me a peculiarly drab way of traveling, whether through a city or through a life. The automated voice calling out directions as you go may mean that you never have to find your way again, but it exacts a heavy toll. The route becomes just a line, the straighter the better. The surrounding landscape becomes irrelevant. There's no wandering off the designated path because something looks interesting—no chance of spontaneity, no adventure. What happens is strictly according to plan. But even as you plan for security, ignoring Robert Burns's warning that "the best laid schemes of mice and men go oft awry," you leave no room for the original meaning of happiness. Before it got corrupted into a psychological commodity, "happiness" was a variant of "hap," as in fortune or chance (think of the word happenstance, for instance, or hapless, or perhaps). This was not an ideal or a goal, nor something that could be deliberately sought out, let alone purchased. It was a state of being: a matter of openness—to the fortuitous, to the unexpected, to moments of grace.

Without the willingness to find yourself lost, as it were, you won't make mistakes, but you won't make discoveries either. The journey is strictly routine. I can drive across the USA from the Atlantic to the Pacific in two or three days if I have to, in an interstate-induced daze. I will never be lost; I will always know where I am. But this "where" will not be in terms of place—one place name on an exit sign becomes as meaningless as the next. Instead, it will be a constant series of calculations: time and distance traveled, hours and miles to go. It will be a journey made in the abstract. I have crossed the continent this way three times, and it is every bit as tiresome and tiring as it sounds. In the rush to get from one point to another, everything in between—life itself—gets lost.

So, you might say, does God. Or rather, the intuition of the transcendent that is personified and thus diminished by that capitalized name. When we name something, we lay claim to it, like Adam and Eve naming the animals in the garden, and can thus imagine that we establish order and control. But naming is a far trickier business than at first appears. Names pin things down, confining them to a graspable conceptual space. They make things deceptively solid and thus create the illusion of understanding. Which is why naming God might be the trickiest business of all.

If there is one thing that can really be said with any certainty about God, it is that the name is utterly insufficient to the concept. What, then, if we were to refrain from laying claim to it? What if we were to drop the pretense of familiarity, the hubris of claiming to know the unknowable and trying to nail down the transcendent? What, that is, if we were to leave God out of the discussion—not as a matter of disbelief, but in full awareness of the insufficiency of the name, and in acknowledgment of whatever it is that we sense it might stand for?

The idea of that temple to the *agnostos theos* stays with me. Sometimes I wish I could have seen it, but that's only in a touristy hey-look-at-that kind of way. In truth

I'm glad I can't, because any attempt to enclose the unknown in a pillared, porticoed building surely defeats its purpose. The soaring arches of temples, cathedrals, and grand mosques are magnificent, but they leave me all too aware of how my experience has been framed and determined by the architects. There's an inherent paradox in trying to express infinity by enclosing space. By building walls, we shut out mystery; we enclose ourselves in belief, in the illusion of knowing.

THREE | IN DOUBT WE TRUST

"I CAN'T BELIEVE YOU DON'T

believe in ANYTHING!!!!!" I'd posted some preliminary thoughts on what it could mean to be agnostic, and this is how one reader responded, the capital letters and exclamation marks conveying her wail of disbelief.

For a moment I felt oddly guilty. This had come from someone who evidently believed in me—trusted me, that is. But what kind of human being could I claim to be if I didn't believe in anything at all? A nihilist? A moral coward? A godforsaken creature left to the whims and mercies of fate? Then I realized that she had misplaced the emphasis. It belonged not on belief, but on the deceptively small word that followed it.

There are indeed many things that I believe, but without the insistence that I believe *in* them, and with the hard-won and still-easy-to-ignore awareness that I might be wrong. It would make sense, for instance, to ask if I believed the latest news report, since the news is not always reliably sourced. But it would be absurd to ask if I believed *in* the news. I may believe specific reporters to be reliable, but I also acknowledge the possibility that they may sometimes be mistaken. As may I. There's an extent to which I choose what to believe, so that I'll have a harder time believing something that runs counter to my preconceptions and expectations, whether acknowledged or unacknowledged. Like most people, I can be obstinately resistant to reality.

Under mortar fire in Jerusalem on June 5, 1967, I drove panicked parents to find their children, zigzagging as shells exploded on either side of the road and staying calm by telling myself that it was all unreal. "It's just like in the movies," I kept thinking. Decades later, my capacity for denial was no less robust. "No, that can't be happening," I said as I watched what was happening in lower Manhattan the morning of September 11, 2001, from a safe three thousand miles away. "Those aren't people falling . . ." And even as the television screen filled with that vast cloud of dust and debris and the news anchors announced with horror that the first tower had collapsed, I stubbornly insisted that they were exaggerating, only to be stunned into silence as the second tower also fell.

Reality may require acceptance, but it does not require belief. Indeed, belief—or as in my case that terrible September morning, disbelief—can be what stands in the way of accepting reality. It can even be an outright rejection of what's real, as it is with climate-change deniers, who bring to mind Montaigne's sharp observation that "we believe nothing so firmly as what we least know."

Sociobiologists have argued that humans have an innate bias toward belief as a matter of physical survival. A prehistoric hunter would have been wiser to take a rustling in the forest as ominous than to blithely trust it was not. Or, in more familiar terms, better safe than sorry. If this theory means that I would not have lasted long in a prehistoric forest, I can live with that. But it may also go some way toward explaining why so many people long for certainty; why they experience uncertainty as an unpleasant state of being, as though a saber-toothed tiger were waiting to pounce; and why, despite the occasional criticism of someone as credulous and thus liable to believe anything at all, the idea that belief is good seems built into the way we think.

Someone may be praised as being true to his beliefs, for instance, as though the act of belief were a value in itself, a moral stance, no matter the content of the belief in question. In matters of religion, belief can even develop into something of a full-time occupation—a profession, in both senses of the word. You don't simply believe; you become a believer. You are defined by living in the state of belief, both in the eyes of others and in your own. Belief can then develop into an impassioned state of being where the act of believing is more important than its content, which is why the most ardent fundamentalists can turn into the most vehement atheists, flaming red socialists into deep-blue conservatives, hedonists into ascetics (and all, by the same token, potentially vice versa).

At first glance, there appears to be great security in being a believer—the security of one's convictions, as they say. We tend to admire people of strong convictions (especially when theirs tally with our own). Indeed, there are times when even the most resolute agnostic might wistfully think of conviction as enviable, a refuge from the hard work of thought. Until, that is, you find yourself up against the stone wall of someone whose "mind is made up," a phrase that makes me think of an army cot in barracks, with the corners folded down so tight that you have to struggle to get into it. Everything is squared away: no soft folds, no creases, no loose ends, the blanket pulled so taut that you can bounce a coin off it. This is a mind wrapped tight, like a mummy. Let no questions enter here.

The more firmly I hold a belief (and note that word hold, that sense of possession, of its being *mine*), the more liable it is to fossilize into conviction, as tightly constricted as that army cot, or as a convict in his cell. And when my belief is so adamantly held that it becomes central to my identity, your disbelief then undermines not only the assumed truth of what I believe, but *me*.

This is no mere schoolyard "I am right and you are wrong." Instead, it is "I am right and you are wrong, and your wrongness is a threat to my identity." Or even to my existence. As Samuel Johnson put it in rather more elegant terms: "Every man who attacks my belief diminishes in some degree my confidence in it, and therefore makes me uneasy; and I am angry with him who makes me uneasy."

To be secure in one's convictions is thus to be absurdly oxymoronic, since conviction is really a state of insecurity. If you know something for a fact, you have no need to believe it or to be convinced of it. You need belief only when you are not sure. Belief is thus the product not of knowledge, but of uncertainty. It contains within itself the possibility of disbelief.

If I gird myself in the psychic armor of righteousness, it is precisely because on some level, conscious or not, I am aware of my vulnerability. Why else would I need any kind of armor? As with the stiff gait of an elderly arthritic person, the tenacious rigidity of conviction indicates not strength, but frailty. Or perhaps it is an evasion of a deeper, more complex, and far more challenging response to uncertainty, which is to embrace it.

ONE OF THE MOST STUNNING examples of religious doubt comes from a man many people might think the last to exhibit it: Muhammad. As told in the earliest Islamic biographies, the foundation moment of Islam—the night Muhammad received the first Quranic revelation on Mount Hira, just outside Mecca—is shot through with soul-rending doubt. Where you might expect the newly anointed prophet to be in a state of elation, floating down the mountain as though walking on air, what you find is quite the opposite. In his own reported words, Muhammad was convinced at first that what had happened couldn't have been real.

At best, he thought, it had to have been a hallucination—a trick of the eye or the ear, perhaps, or his own mind working against him. At worst, he'd been seized by an evil jinn, a spirit out to deceive him, even to crush the life out of him. In fact he was so sure that he could only be *majnun*—possessed by a jinn—that when he found himself still alive, his first impulse was to finish the job himself, to leap off the highest cliff and escape the terror of what he'd experienced, by putting an end to all experience.

Muhammad did not float down that mountain; he fled down it, trembling not with joy but in fear for his sanity. And if this reaction strikes us now as unexpected, even shockingly so, that is only a reflection of how badly we have been misled into demonizing doubt and idolizing belief.

The sheer humanness of Muhammad's disbelief may

be the strongest argument for the historical reality of that night. Whether you think the words he heard came from outside him or from inside—a matter of divine revelation or of human inspiration—it seems clear that he did indeed experience them, and with a force that would shatter his sense of himself and his world, and eventually transform this seemingly ordinary man into an extraordinary one. Fear and denial seem the only sane reaction—the only human reaction. Too human, it appears, for conservative Muslim scholars, who maintain that the account of Muhammad wanting to kill himself should be quashed, no matter how revered the sources. They insist that he never doubted for even a single moment, let alone despaired. Demanding perfection, they refuse to tolerate what they see as human imperfection.

Yet what, exactly, is imperfect about doubt? As I read those early accounts, it was precisely Muhammad's doubt that brought him alive for me, that allowed me to accord him the integrity of reality. Doubt made him human, and his humanity made him real. And yet doubt has a terrible reputation, even among its advocates.

Here's Voltaire, for instance: "Doubt is not a pleasant condition, but certainty is an absurd one." While this may seem satisfyingly witty at first glance, however, it's not quite there. The author of the satirical *Candide* was as subject as anyone else to things-taken-for-granted, among them the idea that doubt is necessarily unpleasant. Though not nearly as unpleasant as it apparently was for Saint Augustine, who wrote of his conversion moment, "There was infused in my heart something like the light of full certainty, and all the gloom of doubt vanished away."

Metaphors don't come much more loaded than this. Light and joy on the one hand, darkness and gloom on the other. Yet Augustine's image of the "gloom of doubt" has sunk deep into the way we think. We have been made so fearful of doubt that we treat it as a character flaw, if not an outright enemy. In John Milton's epic poem *Paradise Lost*, a vengeful Satan sows the seeds of doubt as though it were an invasive species taking over and destroying the carefully cultivated garden. We are still apt to declare that we believe something "beyond all shadow of a doubt," thus casting doubt as an ominous dark cloud in the blue sky of conviction. Under stress, we may doubt our senses, as Muhammad did that night on the mountain, or doubt the evidence of our own eyes.

We even speak of someone being plagued, tormented, or racked by doubt—subjected to the psychic equivalent of medieval torture, with the limbs of the mind stretched beyond endurance.

But is Augustine's "light of full certainty" really preferable? Something about it makes me think of the proverbial light at the end of the tunnel: the light of the oncoming train, that is. Such certainty terrifies me. I recognize it in fanatics and fundamentalists of all religious stripes, in gurus and demagogues and dictators, in all those utterly convinced of their own rightness, their own inerrancy. In fact I find it hard—make that impossible—to trust anyone who never experiences doubt.

THOSE I KNOW of deepest faith are not convinced. "Perfect faith" is a cruel and absurd oxymoron so far as they are concerned. Their minds are not made up, and their faith offers anything but smug self-satisfaction. Indeed they have faith not only despite their doubts, but precisely because of them. They have made a commitment to faith, not in the assurance that they are right and that they have found or possess the truth—the consumerist approach to religion—but in the acknowledgment of how much cannot be known, and how presumptuous it is to imagine that everything can be. They do not claim to have all the answers, or worse, *the* answer. Instead, they have a deep sense of unknowability, of the ineffable mystery of existence referred to in metaphysical shorthand as God.

There is nothing restful about real faith. Where belief is the easy way out, a comfortable position for pious couch potatoes, faith demands an active engagement with uncertainty. "Doubt," wrote playwright John Patrick Shanley in the introduction to his drama of that name, "requires more courage than conviction does, and more energy; because conviction is a resting place and doubt is infinite—it is a passionate exercise." An exercise of the heart, that is, as much as of the mind—not of one against the other, but of the two interwoven, each constantly challenging and thus enriching the other.

As Graham Greene indicated in his novels of those struggling with faith, doubt is the heart of the matter. It is what keeps religion human, because when doubt is banished, faith is rendered moot. Abolish all doubt,

and what's left is not faith, but absolute, heartless conviction, a blind and blinding refuge from both thought
and humanity. You are certain that you possess "the
Truth"—inevitably offered with that uppercase T—and
this certainty easily devolves into dogmatism and righteousness: a demonstrative, overweening pride in being
so very right. You occupy this assumed truth, stake it out
as your exclusive territory, and see all who live beyond
its borders as a threat. Then you add insult to injury by
loudly insisting that in this, you and you alone are, as
fundamentalists say, "the faithful."

But what a heavily loaded term "faithfulness" is. The
ancient association of religious fidelity with sexual
fidelity still holds sway, as when someone is married to
his beliefs. It's spelled out in the Bible, whose prophets
saw Jerusalem as a harlot "committing adultery" and
"prostituting herself to false gods." The biblical writers
pushed this metaphor to the point of outright pornogra-
phy, though you need to go back to the original to see the
extent of it, because they were censored in translation.
The King James version of Ezekiel 23:20, for instance,
portrays an unfaithful Judea with eye-glazing vagueness as "doted upon by her paramours, whose flesh is as

the flesh of asses, and whose issue is like the issue of horses." The original Hebrew, on the other hand, is startlingly explicit: Judea is "infatuated by licentious lovers with penises as big as those of donkeys, ejaculating as wildly as stallions." Yahweh was indeed a jealous god.

There's a stronger word for unfaithfulness, of course: betrayal. You betray your marital vows or your partner. You cravenly betray your principles, or worse, your country, which is when betrayal ramps up into treason. And when you betray God? Then you get the volatile power of the word infidel, a favorite expletive of Muslim fundamentalists in particular, despite the irony that all Muslims were once condemned as infidels by the Christian fundamentalists known as Crusaders. The language of betrayal apparently loses nothing in its repetitiveness.

What's really being betrayed here, however, is faith itself. To conflate faith with belief is to eviscerate faith, even though the two have been used as virtual synonyms for centuries. Maimonides' thirteen principles of faith, for instance, each begin with "I believe with perfect faith." Or do they? That's how the usual English translation has it, but what he actually wrote was *ani maamin be'emuna shlayma*—"I believe with perfect belief"—a declaration that can be seen, depending on your point of view, either as pure sophistry or as an accurate reflection of the self-involvement of belief.

Where belief tries to expel doubt, faith walks with it, offering no easy answers. Belief insists, while faith hopes and trusts. The one is demanded, the other freely given, and this freedom means that real faith is both difficult and stubborn. It involves an ongoing struggle, a continual questioning of what we think we know, a wrestling with issues and ideas. It goes hand-in-hand with doubt, in a never-ending conversation with it. And sometimes even in conscious defiance of it.

I HAVE FOLLOWED Middle East politics closely ever since my thirteen years in Jerusalem, so I am painfully aware of how absurd I sound when I say that I have faith that peace between Israel and Palestine is possible. Anyone who merely scans the news has to see this as at best naive, at worst downright delusional. And I have no option but to agree, because I cannot say that I actually believe that such a peace is possible. In fact, I'd have to say that based on everything I know—the weight of which feels far too heavy—I believe it to be impossible. Yet I insist nonetheless on its possibility.

This is more than mere stubbornness. On the most pragmatic level, the first step in peace-making is to rid one's mind of Hallmark-card images of doves fluttering up into a blue sky and former enemies falling on each other's shoulders in newly sworn fellowship. Peace is both far harder and far more mundane than that. It starts with the obvious, which proves amazingly hard to see: that it is in the parties' long-term mutual interest to refrain from killing each other no matter what has happened in the past. Not long before he died, political historian Tony Judt wrote that "it ought not to be beyond the intelligence of even the most hidebound local politicians to see the benefits of imaginative compromise." It certainly hasn't been in the past. There's no love lost between England and Germany, for instance, though they're at peace after two utterly devastating wars in just the first half of the twentieth century. And there's less than no love lost between Israel and Egypt, though that peace treaty has held for decades, however uneasily. Yet pragmatism seems so alien a concept as regards Israel and Palestine that even in terms of un-dramatic, everyday peace, I still can't see it. But to then conclude that something is impossible because I can't see it says far more about my own limited vision than about what may happen in the future.

This would be merely my own problem were it not so widespread, and thus so dangerous. What we believe affects how we act. If we believe that Middle East peace is impossible (or even, as in the minds of extremists on either side, undesirable), then we will act in such a way that we make it so. We will create a self-fulfilling prophecy of unending conflict, born of the nihilism of despair. And this I refuse. In the face of the despair that threatens to overwhelm me at the latest news, I have no choice but to insist on the possibility of some form of peace, no matter how unlikely I know that to be.

There are times when we need to be irrational, and go beyond doubt. Times, you might say, of creative irratio-nality. No act of heroism would be possible if rationality were to hold sway and the imperative of self-preservation allowed to override the impulse to aid and assist a stranger. No act of generosity either. Nobody would ever fall in love, or place the interests of those they love above their own. Playing it safe, we would give up experiment and exploration, both physical and intellectual, and stick with what we know. We would be trapped in the zero-sum game known as the prisoner's dilemma, which is set up in such a way—two suspects interrogated separately— that the only logical solution is for each to confess and serve jail time instead of maintaining innocence and going free. We would never dare take a chance.

While rationality weighs probabilities and acts accordingly, creative irrationality weighs them and acts nonetheless. Is that foolhardy? Perhaps. Admirable? Possibly. The only thing certain is that there are no guarantees here, no assurance of reward. If assurance is what you want, then like the two prisoners in the famous dilemma, your sole option is the dead end of conviction.

I insist on the possible, then, however improbable it may be. And I do this not only as a matter of principle but as one of personal survival, because I would not want to live in a predetermined world—the world of millennial nightmares such as that in the Book of Revelation, where everything seems fated, "the end times" are eternally nigh, and there is no point in speaking out. In a world, that is, without hope.

I refuse to call closure on hope. Not blind, delusional hope, but conscious hope against the odds—the kind of hope that allows me to speak, to act, to not cave in to the stone wall of the impossible. If I have to, I will keep banging my head against that wall rather than sit numbly at its foot in the cowed inertia of despair, because despair is the inability to imagine oneself into the future. It is a failure of the imagination—of the human ability to conceive of a different reality, and to act accordingly. By resisting despair, then, I rationally choose to be irrational. I defy my own disbelief. And that, I believe, can only be called an act of faith.

AN AGNOSTIC WITH FAITH? If this sounds like I've fallen prey to the clutches of oxymoron, that may only be because so many of us have assented to the conflation of faith with belief. What faith actually requires is not belief, but the ability to suspend *dis*belief.

The concept comes from Samuel Taylor Coleridge,

who wrote of poetic faith as "the willing suspension of disbelief for the moment," and in doing so, created a defining concept not only of poetry, but of all literature. When I read a good novel I am well aware that what I'm reading is fiction, yet for the time I am in its fictional world, I accept it as real, and that alternate reality stays with me long after I close the book. It resonates with me, feeds back into me, gives me an expanded sense of both my own existence and that of others; it is an exercise in empathy on the part of both writer and reader. Whatever the specific content of a piece of literature, it is part of an ongoing conversation about what it is to be human.

I would go further than Coleridge, however, and say that all faith is essentially poetic, in that it delves beneath the surface of things, creating new meaning beyond what can be baldly stated. Whether secular or religious, it is a statement of trust, even of hope. This is not blind trust, naively given. It offers no guarantees (you may on occasion want to toss that novel out the window after just a few pages). It establishes no proofs. In much the same way that you might place your faith in another person, you can never be sure. You trust, and that is always a risk. But how boring and lonely a life in which nothing is ever risked.

"The power to trust, to risk a little beyond the literal evidence, is an essential function," wrote William James in his essay "The Sentiment of Rationality." Indeed, he added, "we cannot live or think at all without some degree of faith."

I love that statement, and if there were no fundamentalists around, I'd even believe it to be true. But faith—and the vulnerability and humility that come with it—is the most important thing lacking in fundamentalists of all religious stripes. Indeed, their absolutism is the opposite of faith, and this makes them the real infidels. By insisting on absolute belief, they have found the perfect antidote to thought, and the ideal refuge from the hard demands of faith. They don't have to struggle for it like Jacob wrestling through the night with the angel, or like Jesus in his forty days and nights in the wilderness, or like Muhammad—not only that night on the mountain but throughout his years as a prophet, with the Quran constantly urging him not to despair, and condemning those who most loudly proclaim that they know everything there is to know, and that they and they alone are right. Terrified of what existentialist phi-

losopher Søren Kierkegaard famously called "the leap of faith," fundamentalists cling to conviction.

WHAT KIERKEGAARD actually wrote was "the leap *to* faith," a prepositional change that makes the idea seem specifically religious. But faith is not the sole province of religion. It turns out to be as important in science as it is in religion, in the arts, or in any other realm of human thought and endeavor. And every time, it requires that leap into the unknown. So when dogmatic atheists assume that science has all the answers, or imagine that it soon will, they are no more immune than the most literal religious fundamentalist to the deceptive enchantment of certainty. In effect, they take the name of science in vain, because faith—along with its partner, doubt—is as essential to science as it is to religion. Or rather, as essential to good science as it is to good religion.

From Einstein on, leading scientists have emphasized the vital role of doubt and uncertainty in their work, and they have done so with passion. "Doubt is not an obstacle to understanding," Nobel laureate Richard Feynman once remarked to fellow physicist Freeman Dyson. "It is the essence of understanding." In fact, Feynman wrote, "It is imperative in science to doubt. It is absolutely necessary to have uncertainty as a fundamental part of your inner nature . . . The statements of science are not of what is true and what is not true, but of what is known to different degrees of certainty. Every one of the concepts of science is on a scale graduated somewhere between, but at neither end of, absolute falsity and absolute truth."

Columbia University neuroscientist Stuart Firestein actually uses the taboo word ignorance, arguing for its creative value as the driving force of science. "Being a scientist," he says, "requires having faith in uncertainty, finding pleasure in mystery, and learning to cultivate doubt. There is no surer way to screw up an experiment than by being sure of its outcome."

I know nothing about Firestein's religious beliefs or absence thereof, but if I believed that such a thing as perfection was possible, then "having faith in uncertainty" would be a perfect definition of what it is to be agnostic. "Mucking about in the unknown is an adventure," he continues, "and doing it for a living is something most scientists consider a privilege . . . They don't stop at the facts; they begin there, right beyond the facts, where the facts run out." This is not to say that Firestein has any patience for what he calls "that callow indifference to facts or logic that shows itself as a stubborn devotion to uninformed opinions" (witness: climate-change denial). Instead, he uses the term "knowledge-able ignorance," a concept guaranteed to craze those who yearn for answers that stay firmly in place.

Just the names of some of the major paradigms of modern physics can drive fundamentalists up the wall, or at least further up the wall than usual. Einstein's two theories of relativity, Heisenberg's uncertainty principle, and Gödel's incompleteness theorems are all part of a world where things-once-taken-for-granted are up for grabs. When photons appear to be both waves and particles at the same time, what once seemed as objectively solid as a billiard ball is revealed as elusively insubstantial. It's not the certainty of science that fundamentalists find intolerable but its uncertainty—the knowledge that no knowledge is absolute. And in this they are not alone.

Those who nurture the illusion that the role of science is to dispel uncertainty and doubt are equally liable to find the shifting quality of knowledge intolerable.

"Scientific materialists," Einstein called them, doomed to settle for "uninspired empiricism." As he saw it, "both the fanatical atheists and the religious fanatics are creatures who can't hear the music of the spheres." Cursed with a tin ear for both science and life, they remain indifferent to "something subtle, intangible, and inexplicable" beyond the limits of what can be observed.

Einstein found the inexplicable to be anything but frustrating; indeed, he found it exhilarating. "Without a preoccupation with the eternally unattainable in the field of art and scientific research," he wrote in his final years, "life would have seemed empty." What concerned him was not the life of the spirit—that constricting definite article again—but life *with* spirit.

Again I defer to William James, this time riffing on what to my mind is one of the most intriguing words in the English language: maybe. James saw this not just as an honest response to the unknown, but as an invitation into it. "So far as man stands for anything and is productive or originative at all," he wrote, "his entire vital function may be said to have to deal with maybes. Not a victory is gained, not a deed of faithfulness or courage is done, except upon a maybe."

This is the agnostic's faith: not in answers, but in possibilities. It's in the way doubt opens up thought instead of closing it off—in the vitality of a mind intrigued, challenged, dancing with uncertainty instead of being plagued by it. That is why, as an agnostic, I place my faith in inquiry. Or as Emily Dickinson poetically put it, "I dwell in possibility."

FOUR | **MYSTERY PLAY**

WHEN A RESOLUTE AGNOSTIC

decides to spend the night alone on top of Mount Sinai, the question has to be why. "Because it's there," said George Mallory when asked in 1923 why he was determined to climb Everest. But while that may have been an apt response to the popular desire for neat explanations, it remains insufficient. Not everything is given to explanation, neat or otherwise. "What's it like to spend the night on top of a sacred mountain?" was not a rational question, yet I'd asked it nonetheless. Was I just another slave to the metaphor of heavenly height?

I'd heard many of the devotional stories that seemed to hover around this mountain: tales of divine manifestations and of holy figures famous and less famous, like the hermit Saint Onuphrios, his beard flowing down to his toes to cover his nakedness as he spoke with angels in his cave. I'd also heard the adjectives trotted out to describe the impact of mountains on the human mind—sublime, majestic, awe-inspiring—so many times that they seemed to lose all meaning. I pushed back against the weight of others telling me what I should feel, trying to predetermine what I saw. But I perked up when I learned that both Christian and Muslim traditions forbade sleeping on the mountain. Transgression? That made the idea irresistible.

This wasn't the first time I'd climbed to the peak. I'd been up before with others, starting at dawn on the direct route: the thirty-one hundred steeply stepped boulders heaved into place by medieval monks from the monastery of Santa Katerina at the foot of the mountain. But now, instead of the steps, I took a roundabout back way, a narrow trail worn into the rock by goats and ibex, so that nobody would try to stop me.

I knew this may not have been the "real" Mount Sinai—the biblical one ascended by Moses and by Elijah after him, the one where Yahweh reportedly spoke to his prophets. It's not even the highest mountain in the Sinai range. The nearby peak of Jebel Katerina is higher but not as clearly delineated as this one, which is set apart on three sides by deep ravines and on the fourth by a small, sandy plain where you could, if you were so inclined, imagine the Israelites camped out with their golden calf. If you take the biblical account of the Exodus literally, however, this would have been a strange diversion. Why head for the mountains in the south when a direct route to the north would have made more sense? But there are no mountains in northern Sinai, let alone one as suitably majestic as this high-walled mound of red granite with its jagged black volcanic peak. And so from the third century on, hermits (and then, when there were too many hermits to merit the name any longer, monks) decided that this place fit the bill. Human desire blended with topography to make it "the" mountain. And this meant that however alone I might be that night, my experience would inevitably be mediated by the long human history of the place. Which was apparently what I wanted.

The steeper the trail became, the more aware I was of my own heartbeat, my body busily proclaiming its vitality in a landscape that seemed inimical to life. I felt small and vulnerable, and that was both frightening and exhilarating; the fear gave an edge to the exhilaration, sharpening it as I gained height and the trail became more challenging. Red granite is a harsh surface to climb on at the best of times, and the rock was hot with the late-afternoon sun, so by the time I reached a narrow defile not far below the peak, weary legs and sore feet made me grateful for the promise of shade.

Too much shade, perhaps. It was only when I entered the defile that I realized just how narrow it was, and how deep. Its darkness felt ominous, as though this were not merely forbidding but forbidden territory. I took a few tentative steps forward, fighting a moment of panic as the rock walls appeared to close in on me and the thought flashed through my head that I'd be trapped here, that the stone would never let me out. And then I found myself moving into something ineffably strange and uncannily beautiful: a deep rose-colored light that seemed to come from everywhere and nowhere. The air itself was suffused with this light, glowing with it, and as I breathed in, it seemed to suffuse me too. I felt like I was floating, buoyed by the light, cradled and gentled by it. It was as though the mountain was welcoming me, taking me into itself, and even as some part of me was aware that this was an absurd notion, it was almost palpable nonetheless.

It lasted perhaps a minute or two, no more. At the far end of the defile, the steep rock walls fell away and the light subsided, mellowing into the old-master colors of early sunset as I found myself looking over the hollow hidden at the heart of the mountain—Elijah's Hollow, the bedouin call it—and just below me, the final reach of steep bouldered steps up to the peak. I remember thinking that I should turn back and figure out what had caused that extraordinary light. And yet I didn't. Some part of me was afraid that if I did, the light wouldn't be there anymore; another part, that I'd discover the cause and thus explain the light away. I didn't turn back, because I didn't want reason or causality. I opted instead for mystery. I sat down and stayed there a while, reveling in what felt like my own magic mountain, and then went on, up to the peak and the sunset spreading gold then red and then purple over the mountains, and finally the ethereal silver of moonlight.

HOWEVER SECULAR I think I may be, the cultural and historical weight of religion bears down on me. It haunts the imagination. I only have to hear the first chanted words of the kaddish, the Jewish prayer for the dead, for chills to start up and down my spine. The tolling of the cathedral bell at Easter, the call of the muezzin at dawn, the blowing of the shofar on Yom Kippur—some part of me responds to them even as another part asks what I think I'm doing. Ritual strikes deep, reaches beyond the intellect. Gregorian chants, Bach's Mass in D Minor, the soaring voice of the great Sufi singer Nusrat Fateh Ali Khan—all resonate somewhere beyond reason. As does "Taps," the lone bugle melody played at U.S. military funerals. "Day is done," go the lyrics, "gone the sun, from the lakes, from the hills, from the sky. All is well, safely rest, God is nigh." The words alone make me hear the bugle, and the sound of it makes me want to cry.

Does this make me a romantic, or merely a sentimentalist? Am I really no more than a patsy of religiously infused culture? When I think back to that defile on Mount Sinai, I realize that perhaps what I'm really asking is this: Can a firmly secular person have a religious experience? To which my answer is yes, of course she can, because that qualifier "religious" is added on ex post facto; it refers not to the experience itself, but to an interpretation of that experience. This happened on Mount Sinai, for God's sake, so it had to be religious, right? If not a full-scale revelation, at least an awakening, an opening of the eyes, as in "I saw the light."

That's literally true, but let's leave the definite article out of it. I saw light, and it was both unnerving and beautiful. But to extrapolate from that and say that I saw *the* light is to assume meaning. The definite article overdetermines the matter. As I sat resting before going on up to the peak, I was certainly aware that what had happened was quite perfect—exactly the sort of thing that *should* happen on a holy mountain. Prepped for mystery by all the stories I knew, I opted out of verification and went with the vision of the moment and the place. And this was my conscious choice.

It was a Romantic poet, John Keats, who described breaking free of prescriptive systems of thought and perception as "negative capability." This is the capacity, he said, to be "in uncertainties, mysteries, doubts, without any irritable reaching after fact and reason." I'm not sure why he thought of it as negative, but his choice of that word "irritable" works for me. It makes me think of the way a dinner table comes to life when something intriguing arises in the conversation—a sighting of what might have been a sundog, perhaps, or a half-remembered quote teasing the memory—only for someone with the fact-checking impulse to pull out his phone, check it out on Google or Wikipedia, read aloud what he's found, and then sit there triumphantly as though waiting for applause. Instead, there's a dull hiatus. A pall descends over the conversation as the pleasure of speculation comes up against the assumed authority of explanation. Fact and reason have been placed against mystery and enchantment, and there's an unspoken resentment at the intrusion.

The issue here isn't what happened to me on Mount Sinai, but how I think about what happened. I could always give in to the relentless need to categorize, to file something neatly under the appropriate tag and move on to whatever comes next. I could tell my story slightly differently as a mystical or a spiritual experience, however self-aggrandizing that might be. I could plead physiology and say that I was suffering from mild dehydration, since I'd carried less water with me than I should have and thus rationed myself, which is unwise in the desert. I could point to simple physics: a matter of refraction, with the light of the lowering sun angled just so, bouncing off the red granite and intensifying in that narrow space. Or I could say that I was in an altered state of consciousness caused by altitude and weariness, though that seems disappointingly down-to-earth for such a heady state of mind, and how down-to-earth does anyone want to be when they're up on top of a mountain?

A WHOLE WALL in my local library is labeled "Mysteries." Most of the books are detective stories, a safe, elementary-my-dear-Watson form of mystery, where I know before I even open the cover that all will eventually be revealed. Each volume offers a frisson of fear— the tense excitement of coming face-to-face with the incomprehensible, even the impossible, like the murdered man found in a room locked from the inside. But only a frisson, since the fear is tempered with the knowledge that there will, in the end, be a rational explanation. The uncanny will be revealed as canny, the unknowable knowable. Yet I can't help feeling a certain disappointment when, with a few honorable exceptions (Nicolas Freeling's *Wolfnight* comes to mind, as does Per Wahlöö's *Murder on the Thirty-first Floor*), the "reveal" arrives in the last few pages. The detailed exposition of whodunnit, and how and why they dunnit, has a distinctly anticlimactic feeling. What kept me reading was the pleasure of everything *not* making sense; I took delight in the suspense, and now, faced with the answer to it all, I feel let down, brought back to earth from my escapist enjoyment. Does anyone with a memory read any such novel twice?

When the uncanny remains uncanny, though, it is no longer merely a puzzle to be solved. It becomes supernatural, and thus enters the realm of religious experience, whether defined as such or not. That is what makes Henry James's novella *The Turn of the Screw* so haunting (no coincidence that he was William James's brother). It was also the impulse behind Mary Shelley's creation of

Frankenstein and his monster. "I busied myself to think of a story which would speak to the mysterious fears of our nature and waken thrilling horror," Shelley wrote later, "one to make the reader dread to look around, to curdle the blood and quicken the beatings of the heart." What she came up with was a kind of inverse ghost story in which the human is haunted not by the dead, but by the horribly living. By reaching for God-like knowledge of creation, Frankenstein transgressed what was taken to be the natural order of things, which was understood as divinely given.

This sense of transgression is at the heart of all ghost stories, where the dead are undead, and the living appalled. Shakespeare made shrewd use of the uncanny when he opened one of his greatest plays with a ghostly appearance, one that chills and thrills with the sense of "more things in heaven and earth, Horatio, than are dreamt of in your philosophy." What makes ghosts so uncanny is precisely their canniness; unworldly beings, they are worldly-wise. They are a conundrum, which is why nobody asks if you believe that ghosts are real; they ask if you believe *in* ghosts, in the same way they ask if you believe in God. Yet even those who don't believe can't help feeling uneasy when they hear ghost stories, which take place in darkness and are told in darkness, whether around a dying campfire or in the dim light of a theater. That quickened heartbeat, the hairs of the neck standing on end, the shivers up and down your spine are all signs of adrenaline flowing in the fight-or-flight response. The felt boredom of the mundane disappears, and the smallest details—the creak of a stair, the banging of a shutter, a sudden draft—sharpen into significance, making you feel more alert, more alive.

"More alive"? The phrase is in much the same realm as "almost pregnant." More *aware* of being alive, then: a matter of consciousness, not of simple physical existence. Or more specifically, a matter of meta-consciousness: the consciousness of being conscious. But how meta can one be and still lead a normal life? As Virginia Woolf noted, most of the day is necessarily buried in a kind of perceptual cotton wool, where routine rules and one thing blurs into another. But then, she argued, there are "moments of being"—moments that stand out sharply, flaring to life with almost cinematic clarity and breaking through that cotton wool of the mundane. And while tragic moments stand out this way, so too do profound moments of love, understanding, and connectedness, suffused with a feeling of intense tenderness.

To be profoundly moved is to move "beyond oneself" (thus the word ecstasy, which comes from the Greek *ek-stasis*, being out of one's usual place). It is to experience, however fleetingly, a sense of being that is grander, wiser, more open, more generous, more whole-hearted and connected to everything and everyone around you. A wide-eyed father listening for the first time to the heartbeat of his child in his wife's womb, for instance; strangers hugging each other in celebration, as many did the morning after electing the first black American president; the sudden and unexpected tears that well up when we see others in tears—these are times when we're no longer merely observers, but part of a "something larger" sensed but not defined.

The experience of wilderness can be equally profound. When I stand by a mountain stream and watch salmon, sluggish with exhaustion after the long journey upriver from the ocean, spawn and then die, I am stunned at this biological imperative, this built-in insistence on creating new life on the brink of death. And

I am nothing less than awed when I make my way to the Pacific shore as a gale sends billions of tons of water pounding across thousands of miles of ocean. The waves crash so powerfully that the ground vibrates beneath my feet, and their force registers on earthquake monitors miles inland. Wind-borne spume fills my vision so that I can no longer tell the difference between earth and water and sky, and I am equal parts terrified and thrilled by such inhuman power.

Such moments can feel intensely physical, as though your heart were literally expanding inside your chest, reaching out into the world around you. "The whole body seems to feel beauty . . . entering not by the eyes alone, but equally through all one's flesh like radiant heat," wrote Sierra Club founder John Muir, the godfather of environmentalism, during the first summer he spent in Yosemite. As with the experience of orgasm, it is an all-encompassing surrender of both mind and body to the place and the moment, which is why Bernini's famed statue of Saint Teresa in ecstasy is so blatantly sexual; why the Sufi poetry of Jalal ad-Din Rumi is intoxicated with lovers' kisses; why the Bible's Song of

Solomon bursts with sensual images; and why those "taken by the spirit" in revivalist tent meetings writhe so suggestively. The evangelicals who made a best-selling franchise of "the Rapture" knew what they were about.

We can heighten this sense—many do—with psychoactive drugs like LSD or MDMA (aptly known as ecstasy), while religious rites in several parts of the world still involve the consumption of psychedelic plants such as peyote and ayahuasca. Whether you think of their use as opening Aldous Huxley's "doors of perception" or as simply enhancing sensation, such drugs really do alter your consciousness. And it takes astonishingly little to do that. A mere drop of liquid on a tab of paper, and you can glimpse infinity in something as simple as the long stretch of a cat's yawn, or, per William Blake, in a grain of sand.

Any number of ambitious names have been coined for this state of being. Freud called it oceanic consciousness; psychologist Abraham Maslow named it peak experience; theologist Rudolf Otto went for the arcane with terms such as the *mysterium tremendum* and numinous consciousness. Religious mystics of all stripes have called it union with the divine, and have learned to induce it without chemical aid through meditation, fasting, ritual movement, chanting, breath control, and, of course, prayer, which when done with intention is itself a form of breath control. An incantation spoken as a slow, measured exhalation into the air around you, prayer combines the doubled meaning of breath and spirit. "Breathe into me," Rumi implored, as though taking inspiration literally. Drunk on love and longing for "the touch of spirit on the body," he resisted all attempts to confine his vision to what he called "that old trickery and hypocrisy" of dogma.

Mysticism is the religious impulse on acid, as it were—anarchic, beholden to no rules. It's the power of ecstasy over sobriety, of inner experience over outward conformity, of intuition over formulaic belief. And while many people find this threatening and do their best to close themselves off from such experience, the capacity for it seems to be built into every one of us, no matter how we define ourselves in religious or secular terms. At least I hope it is. Whether you think of such states of being as union with God or with a lover, with nature or with humanity, there's a great beauty in them. They make us feel more open to the world, less alone in it. They enhance our appreciation of the very fact of our existence. And if this is illusory, it may be a necessary illusion.

THERE'S A CERTAIN bleakness to the purported rule of reason. It's possible, sometimes, to see too clearly. When restorers removed centuries of grime from the ceiling of the Sistine Chapel, they revealed Michelangelo's palette as more primary than previously thought. The grime had obscured the frescoes, hiding detail, but it had also created a mellowing gloss. Without that gloss, many felt as though the ceiling was suddenly in the full glare of the midday sun instead of the gentle glow of candlelight; they missed the patina that obscured vision and yet somehow enhanced it.

We might praise someone as being clear-sighted, but psychological research indicates that this may not be such a great thing. In what's been dubbed depressive realism, people who are depressed may actually see things more realistically than those who are not. If so, then most of us turn out to be true to the metaphor of viewing the world through rose-tinted glasses (was I wearing them when I saw that light on the mountain?), and this could be essential to maintaining sanity on what can sometimes seem an increasingly insane planet.

How clearly is it possible to see? Can we ever grasp things the way they "really" are? One of the leading philosophers of consciousness, Thomas Nagel, has been posing variants of this question ever since his 1974 article "What Is It Like to Be a Bat?," in which he concluded that no matter how much we may know *about* bats—how they fly, how they navigate, and so on—we cannot know the experience of actually being one. Stuck within our own subjectivity, we can only glimpse the radical objectivity of what he called "the view from nowhere."

Few have the intellectual fortitude of someone as ambitiously clear-sighted as Spinoza, who tried to bring the precision of logic to his view of the natural world itself as God, void of intent or of any human attribute at all. Yet much as I admire Spinoza for his courage in battling the idea of the anthropomorphic God—and this did indeed take immense courage in the seventeenth century—I also feel sorry for him. At least he was not burned at the stake for his thinking, as astrologer

Giordano Bruno had been just a few decades earlier, but it was probably inevitable that he was excommunicated for his pains, condemned to a lonely life shut up in a dark room grinding optical lenses—a cruelly ironic occupation for someone so bent on seeing clearly, since it would cost him both his health and his life, dead at forty-four from silicosis caused by inhaling glass dust. How much clarity can any one person stand?

The view, being a view, is always from somewhere. And that being so, where else but from within ourselves? We might strive for clarity, but if we do, the first step is surely to be aware of how fallible the human viewpoint can be. What is experienced is not necessarily what's there. A famous psychological test uses a flashing series of photographs to show how white people with racial bias are more likely to mistakenly see a black person as holding a gun. Memories have been revealed as malleable, highly suggestible and thus unreliable, which is why eyewitness testimony is no longer considered as definitive as it once was, and why line-ups can result in false positive identifications. What we see or remember seeing is often the result of what we expect to see or think we should have seen. It's determined not by the eye but by the mind, which interprets what the eye registers.

Visitors to Yosemite now brave traffic jams and try to square what's in front of them with the dramatic photographs of Ansel Adams, apparently unaware that he spent days and even weeks at a time waiting for just the right light—the luminous quality of "Nature's cathedral," as John Muir called it. Across the world, pilgrims in Jerusalem flock to the Via Dolorosa, shoving elbows as they try to match the biblical city of miracles with the contentious political reality of the twenty-first century, which could certainly use a miracle or two. Whether in California or the Middle East, you'd think such attempts doomed to failure, and yet they're not, because the mind makes good what the eye fails to see. Acting as a kind of built-in Photoshop app, the mind transforms what is seen into what is imagined or remembered. That is, into what it thinks *should* be seen. As with the app, you can adjust tone and contrast, remove imperfections, even create a halo around the image. You can make the visual conform to your narrative of it, which is indeed what artists have always done, long before modern technology.

A nineteenth-century etching by David Roberts hanging by my desk shows a group of tiny figures ascending Mount Sinai. I keep it close even though I know how deceptive it is—or rather, *because* I know. What Roberts drew, with the mountains right before his eyes, was not what his eyes saw, but the image in his mind: the peaks higher, sharper, more dramatic, more in line with his expectation of the majestic and the sublime. Not an empirical representation of reality, that is, but reality transformed by the observer in the light of what he knew about the place. Was this conscious on Roberts's part? I think it had to be. An experienced traveler and highly regarded artist, he did not merely fall under the spell of mystery as though it were cast on him from on high; he actively chose it, in the knowledge that, as William James put it, "the essence of religious experience is at its best poetic."

Ritual and dogma are merely the framework of organized religion. They do not touch on religious experience itself, which is the experience of mystery, of the indescribably enigmatic. And that can also be the experience of science. Einstein sounded as poetic as James when he wrote that "the most beautiful experience we can have is the mysterious. It is the fundamental emotion that stands at the cradle of true art and true science." Seeing the universe as "a great, eternal riddle," he spoke of "the beauty and belief in the logical simplicity of order and harmony that we can grasp only humbly and imperfectly."

When you read James and Einstein side by side, it can sometimes be hard to distinguish which man is speaking: the philosopher or the physicist, the man of religion or the man of science. And this is part of the enduring delight of mystery. It is the realm of ambiguity. Unruly and contradictory, mystery defies the need to adhere to a single narrative and thus "make sense." It refuses to march to the monotonous drumbeat of axioms and assertions taken to be absolute truths. This is why all attempts to control the mysterious and pin it down to a hypothetically correct line, whether in the name of religion or of science, can only fail in the long run, with little to offer but drab against color, factual correctness against awe and wonder, passive acceptance against the active enjoyment—let's not forget enjoyment!—of life itself.

A lovely paradox is at work here. If the sense of mystery is indeed the essence of religious experience, many who do not think of themselves as religious may be more open to such experience than many who do. Blessedly unencumbered by either the need to believe or the need to explain everything, the agnostic is free to experience awe without seeking to define it—to explore and interact with the world in ways that neither the rule-bound fundamentalist nor the dogmatic atheist ever dares dream of.

FIVE | MAKING MEANING

WHAT DO YOU DO WHEN SOMEONE

tells you about a treasured experience that you know is in all probability untrue? True to that person, that is, but not objectively true. I hardly knew the woman who cornered me at a party to tell me about such an experience, but she insisted that my being an accidental theologist made me the perfect audience. She was just back from a trip to the San Juan Islands in the northern part of Puget Sound, and there, she said, the most amazing thing had happened, something she swore had altered her whole way of being.

She'd been standing on a low cliff overlooking one of the narrow straits between the islands, and had seen a pod of orcas. These are perhaps the most photogenic species of whale, elegantly marked in black and white, like large dolphins. Since the San Juans are the breeding ground of several known pods, to see them in these waters was not unusual. What was unusual was that as she watched, the whales lined up in a row, facing the shore, and just hung there for several minutes, singing to her. That was the phrase she used, "singing to me." She knew, she said, that the whales were communicating with her, welcoming her to a larger and more mysterious world than the urban one she had come from. "It was deeply spiritual," she said, "that feeling of connection, like they were sending me a message. It was totally transcendent."

I nodded. I think I used the word beautiful. I chose discretion over honesty, because I had no desire to hurt this person by questioning what was clearly so meaningful to her. There can be great beauty in the enterprise of making meaning, that very human desire to find significance in the world. But it seems to me essential that we be aware that this is what we are doing, and that we retain a certain sense of bemusement, even amusement, at our proclivity to translate the world into human terms. Aware, that is, of our own subjectivity.

While I was not certain why those whales had behaved the way they did, or even if they had lined up and sung as perfectly as the teller remembered—memory, after all, has a way of adapting itself to a desired narrative—I was reasonably sure that it had nothing to do with her presence on the shore. Insofar as whales act with what we think of as intention, the last thing they can have had in mind was the desire to serenade her. Besides, I could conceive of rather more pragmatic reasons for their behavior.

As it happened, I had kayaked that particular stretch of water, so I knew the currents in it and how they change with the tides. The whales might have lined themselves up in the position of least resistance to the current; that is, they might simply have been taking a rest, and the sounds they were making—to human ears, an otherworldly series of squeaks, whistles, and pulses—were sounds of contentment. Or they might have lined up with their backs to some form of underwater disturbance, like military sonar (Puget Sound being home to, among other things, a nuclear submarine base and a naval air base), in which case the sounds may have been a series of distress calls. These pods are among the most closely tracked in the world, yet cetacean researchers still aren't sure how to interpret their behavior. Not that this has been any barrier to either interpretation or commercialization. You can download "whale song" recordings, studio-crafted into humanly recognizable patterns and often marketed as aids to meditation or as suitable accompaniment to a massage. You can adopt a whale, even though this is entirely in principle and the whale in question has the good fortune to know nothing about it. Or you can take a tour boat, see a whale breaching, and swear that its huge eye is staring straight at you and you alone—as will the twenty other people leaning over the railing.

I have nothing against whale-watching, despite its commercialization. If it can turn someone into an environmentalist, I am all for it (provided the boat operators keep a safe distance), and especially so when it becomes a means of acknowledging and respecting other forms of existence. But when it results in someone being convinced that there is a special connection between that utterly other existence and their own, that is something very different.

"The pathetic fallacy," art critic and naturalist John Ruskin called it—the tendency to attribute human emotion and intent to natural phenomena. But while it's certainly a fallacy, I hesitate to call it pathetic in the

modern sense of pitiful. It's unscientific, sure. Sentimental, definitely. Some might call it just another form
of the commodification of nature, the nature-as-theme-
park approach; others might say it's only natural to see
the world this way, since we humans are bound by our
subjectivity. But this projection of the human onto the
non-human also speaks to the desire to go beyond ourselves, even if, paradoxically, it is expressible only in
terms of ourselves. So despite my thinking this person
self-dramatizing in her certainty that she had called
forth a response from the whales, I still found it hard to
naysay. I have seen people destroy the illusions of others, and it is not a pretty sight. I said nothing of my res-
ervations; instead, I thanked her for telling me. And I
did so not only because I had no desire to insult or challenge her experience, but also because I was not at all
sure that I would not have reacted in much the same way.

WHEN I WAS still a graduate student in psychology, I
delved into probability theory with the best in the field,
including a future Nobel laureate. Yet even now, if a coin
were tossed nine times and came up heads each time, I

would be unable to resist betting on its coming up tails the tenth time. What I intuit defies what I know, which is that each toss is independent of the one before, and that the odds are always fifty-fifty. In reality, there is no narrative involved here. The coin has no memory. It doesn't think; I do. And as casino operators know, my thinking is irrational. I find pattern—meaning—where none necessarily exists.

Cultural anthropologist Clifford Geertz famously saw "man as an animal suspended in webs of significance he himself has spun." Woman too. Discerning pattern in what otherwise seems the randomness of everyday life, we interpret chance as significance, contingency as intent. I think I'm not the only one, for instance, who tends to see things happening in sets of three. Two mentions of a movie, a book, or a person I haven't thought about in a while, and I start waiting for the third. Actively waiting, that is, paying attention where otherwise I might not. And while I know that such coincidences are simply instances of directed consciousness, of my mind imposing order on randomness, there's a little thrill of response when they happen. And a certain comfort too. As Geertz indicated, there is something quintessentially human in the aversion to the starkness of chance. As with that tenth toss of the coin, we fall for significance even when reason tells us otherwise. We are suckers for pattern, willing subjects of what is often called "the search for meaning."

Since I have spoken several times at the annual Search for Meaning book festival at Seattle University, a Jesuit college, I may well be accused of a certain lack of grace when I confess what I suspect the Jesuits already know, which is that I have a problem with the search for meaning. Many problems, in fact. Not least among them being the feeling that this is an attempt by religion to co-opt meaning—a semi-secularized rephrasing of "the search for God," or God repackaged, as it were, for those who think of themselves as spiritual-but-not-religious.

I resist thinking of myself as spiritual; the tag feels too nebulous and at the same time too self-congratulatory. But the term has become so widespread that I find myself defined by it nonetheless. It's often assumed that because I study and write about religion (and politics, and existence), I harbor a deep longing for belief. "Ah, you're a seeker," I'm told, which invariably sounds to me like I'm part of a sixties pop group or some new religious order.

The inference strikes me as odd. If I studied crime, for instance, I doubt if many people (with the exception perhaps of strict Freudians) would then assume that I harbor a deep longing to be a criminal. In fact you might say that scholars are the Sherlock Holmeses of religion. Like Sherlock, they notice, investigate, probe, take nothing for granted. They are intellectually engaged observers, and if they are to observe well, a certain detachment is required, as it is with psychotherapists or anthropologists. Yet many people seem to think that the study of religion leaves little room for such detachment. Confusing empathy with sympathy, they mistake understanding for identification. Thus the insistence that there has to be a personal search on my part. Without that, it seems, what excites me or moves me to action or simply gets me out of bed in the morning—what makes me not merely accepting of life, but eager to live it—is somehow lacking a "higher" dimension. It's as though living a politically, socially, and intellectually engaged life is not enough until I find my way to acknowledging some overarching purpose to my existence, one that will grace my every thought and action.

My assumed seeker status is clearly meant in a

kindly way, but I can't help feeling that it's a sort of verbal pat on the head such as an adult might give a bright kid who has just asked an awkward question to which one has no answer. Not only am I thought to be lost (otherwise why would I need to find my way?), but my being lost is understood as distressing. I find myself standing again in front of that lost-and-found department of the soul, where wariness of certainty is interpreted as a pathetic lack of it, and appreciation of unknowability as a sign of ignorance.

But if I am to be considered lost, at least let me be considered happily so. Certainly, as cultural critic Walter Benjamin noted, "not to find one's way in a city may well be uninteresting and banal; it requires ignorance, nothing more. But to lose oneself in a city as one loses oneself in a forest, that calls for quite a different schooling." Essayist Rebecca Solnit took this further in *A Field Guide to Getting Lost* (a title I envied from the moment I first saw it): "To be lost is to be fully present, and to be fully present is to be capable of being in uncertainty and mystery." It becomes the paradoxical art of "being at home in the unknown," she wrote, when "the world has become larger than your knowledge of it." You become conscious, whether with excitement or with fear, that the world does not revolve around you.

THE AWARENESS that humans are not the center of the world still lies uneasily. Science is in many ways an affront to human self-regard. Lit up by the floodlights of our own self-importance (no accident, perhaps, that "lit up" is an old slang term for being drunk), we still tend to claim center stage. We conceive of ourselves as larger than we are, taking up more room in both time and space.

It's been four centuries since Galileo Galilei died under house arrest, "vehemently suspected of heresy" for observing that the sun did not revolve around the earth, but the earth around the sun. That was just forty-two years after Giordano Bruno had been burned at the stake for conceiving of the earth as a speck in an infinite universe. We have so much more perspective now, or at least we think we do. We accept, for instance, that the universe is almost 14 billion years old (13.8 billion, to be more precise, though how much precision there can be in rounding to the nearest tenth of a billion is up for grabs). And yet that statement is inherently false. It is not a statement about the universe, but about us—about the universe, that is, as detected by us. Since the age of what we refer to as the universe is determined by the speed of light reaching earth from the farthest detectable stars, what we detect is essentially a huge sphere with us at its center. Even with the most advanced space telescopes, the universe is defined by the limits of human observation, which is why astrophysicists now temper their language with the addition of a single essential word: "the *observable* universe."

On a more down-to-earth level, the insistence on center stage is dramatized in the schoolbook schematic of the stages of evolution: six evenly spaced steps from knuckle-dragging ape to modern human, with "man" marching purposefully forward as the end point. A realistically proportional timeline would require a page several feet wide until the ambitiously named *Homo sapiens* (literally, wise man) finally appears—though that word finally itself indicates an inevitable progression, even a heroic one. We cast ourselves as the stars of our own existence, and while such self-dramatization may be natural, even inevitable given our subjectivity, it has an unintended consequence: it implies that humans are the goal of evolution. And this is not a scientific idea, but a religious one. A goal assumes prior intent, and science does not assume intent. Religion does, though. It is, in the words of sociologist Peter Berger, "the audacious attempt to conceive of the entire universe as humanly significant."

The pathetic fallacy seems inescapable, especially when you consider what appears to be the extreme improbability of life on earth ever having developed. The smallest deviation one way or another at practically any point over billions of years would have made it impossible. If protons were just 0.2 percent heavier, for example, they'd decay into neutrons unable to hold on to electrons, and there would be no atoms. The odds of our ever having come into being as a species are so minuscule that from an exclusively human point of view, life can seem downright miraculous. And it takes a single leap of logic to then assume not only that the universe is fine-tuned for human life, but that this fine-tuning is a matter of intent. Divine intent, that is. Thus the whole idea of "intelligent design"—a have-it-both-ways ideology whose advocates try to position it as a more intellectually respectable form of creationism. Yet even as it appears to acknowledge evolution, intelligent design denies the underlying principle, which is contingency.

You might think of contingency as the evolution of chance. Human existence may seem miraculous to many people, but to the particles on which it is based, it is merely a matter of physics—of an infinite number of tiny, quantum occurrences. And this is as true on the individual level as it is on the species one. With a minimum of imagination, for instance, I can look back and roughly outline several other lives I might have lived, and might still be living, if I had gone one way or another at this point or that. And each of these is me and yet a different me. I am—we all are—the product of contingency, of possibilities opted for and others turned away from, all of which have brought me to this point in my life, and will incline me one way or another in all the unforeseen points yet to come.

These are not necessarily our own choices. A reflective child discovers the power of contingency as he tries to trace the chain of chance, the particular sequence of small events, each dependent on the one before, that made his existence possible—a bus running late here, a couple of schoolbooks dropped there, any of the multiple tiny occurrences of everyday life that led to a specific woman and a specific man meeting, falling in love, and becoming his mother and father. And if, at any juncture, something else had happened? If the bus had arrived on time, or the schoolbooks been clutched tighter? How humbling to realize that he would not exist.

Contingency is no flatterer of human existence. It involves no values, assigns no particular significance to individual being. It contradicts the human sense of self-importance and centrality, which is why so many people resist it by insisting on significance nonetheless, attributing good or bad fortune to God or to angels, to the stars or to fate. Yet as with the way we tend to see events in groups of three, what we call fortune is usually a matter of directed attention.

Who remembers the time they missed a plane and that same plane did *not* crash, for instance? Or what is the time limit for saying you narrowly escaped being buried in a landslide or caught in a pile-up on a foggy interstate highway? Is it one minute? Five? An hour? A day? ("I was right there just a year ago," I caught myself thinking about a severe earthquake in rural California.)

Such questions have been studied by Yale psychologists, who found that a majority of religious people believe that major events in their lives—accidents, divorce, illness, even the death of those close to them—happen for a reason. This was hardly a surprise. The surprise came when the researchers found that a majority of atheists thought the same, even if they attributed the turn of events to fate instead of divine will. As Rebecca Goldstein succinctly puts it, "the will to matter is at least as strong as the will to believe."

Atheists too, it appears, engage in the search for meaning, striving for significance by rejecting contingency and insisting on life as "something more." And what is that something-more? Psychoanalyst Ernest Becker put it this way: "When the child poses the question 'Who am I? What is the value of my life?' he is really asking something more pointed: that he be recognized as an object of primary value in the universe. Nothing less."

THE IDEA that life should be "worth living" may seem obvious, at least to privileged Westerners who have the time and freedom—the luxury, that is—to insist on value. But what seems obvious can be deceptive. The emphasis on worth proves insidious in its requirement that each of us prove or at least assert our value, even our right to exist. It's a kind of existential capitalism, assuming a marketplace of existence in which some trade at higher prices than others, and in which the values are set not by us but by some outside force, rather like the imagined "hidden hand" of financial markets.

For some, like evangelical pastor Rick Warren, the hidden hand is the hand of God. His popular book *The Purpose Driven Life* (a title that makes me think of type-A personalities driving themselves to cardiac arrest) is peculiarly utilitarian in its assumption that life is something to be used, an instrument to be wielded for some ulterior purpose. The many purposes that each of us finds in love or in work, in thought or in play—and if we are very lucky, in all of the above—are of little interest to him. He's concerned with "ultimate," "higher," "universal" purpose, which he defines as "what God put you on this planet to do." In short, a mission. And not just life *with* a mission, but life *as* a mission.

I am wary of missions, as is perhaps inevitable for a former convent schoolgirl who thought of them as jungle outposts staffed by impossibly self-sacrificing nuns who needed much praying for (though later, I'd think of Graham Greene's tortured whiskey priest in *The Power and the Glory*, and of his blandly righteous "quiet American"). But missions are now big business. From start-ups to major corporations, mission statements are banner-headlined on websites and boosted in television commercials, with the quest for profit disguised in a makeshift costume of moral vision. The aim is "to bring good things to life," "to make a difference," "to impact people's lives," or "to make the earth a better place." A naive observer could easily imagine that such corporations are messianic philanthropists, poised to save the world if only through force of insistence.

Rick Warren's mission is the outsourcing of purpose. Citing the stunningly anthropocentric idea that "the cosmos is a specially designed whole with life and mankind as its fundamental goal and purpose," he concludes that "God designed this planet's environment just so we could live in it." That being just-so, he assures his readers, "God has a purpose for you," and if he never quite specifies exactly what this might be, that makes it all the easier to accept. If purpose is predetermined, you are conveniently relieved of any need to figure out your own. Even as he assigns purpose, then, Warren takes it away, because to outsource responsibility to a divine being is only to diminish the personal sense of responsibility. It's not up to you anymore; it's up to God. And if you are what he calls "an instrument of God," that presumably places you pretty high up on the scale of value.

Wading with conviction into the slippery territory of the meaning of life, Warren capitalizes on a deep unease with the fact that meaning is subjective—not something given, but something constructed. Thomas Nagel gave voice to this unease when he noted that "the universe as revealed by chemistry and physics, however beautiful and awe-inspiring, is meaningless, in the radical sense that it is incapable of meaning." Yet even as apparently rational an observer as Nagel found this ultimately unacceptable. "Existence is something tremendous," he continued, "and day-to-day life, however indispensable, seems an insufficient response to it, a failure of consciousness."

I adore Nagel—how can you not adore a philosopher capable of asking what it's like to be a bat?—but here is where he loses me. Is awareness of the infinite indifference of the universe really a failure of consciousness? Or is the failure that apparent impatience with everyday life? If there is an insufficient response here, it seems to me to be the refusal of the extraordinary grace of chance—the succession of infinitesimally small probabilities that have built on one another to lead to the point where a carbon-based creature could even ask, "What am I doing here?"

Not everything must have meaning. Indeed the Warren-like insistence that everything does, while presented as deeply religious, seems to me fundamentally anti-religious in that it represents a real failure of consciousness: the refusal to accept the sheer, magnificent, mysterious contingency of it all. This, I think, is the point Nagel was making. Such a refusal seems at least churlish, at worst life-denying. By trying to pin down existence as a matter of purpose, Warren diminishes the vital, complex business of actually living day-to-day life.

The absence of an "ultimate" meaning of life—a grand, over-arching explanation of everything—does not render life empty of relevance. On the contrary, it makes it all the more relevant. It means we can no longer use divine intent as an excuse, in the same way fatalists talk of fate. It places responsibility directly on us— responsibility for how we act, for what we do, for our relations with others, with our society, with our planet. It is we who determine meaning by what we do. And part of that meaning is the awareness that we are not and cannot always be in control, that we are indeed subject to chance, to accident, to serendipity, to the unforeseen, the unanticipated, the fortuitous.

I see no reason why meaning and significance should be any less for knowing how vast the universe is, and how small I am in it. Far from being appalled by this, I am excited by it. It allows for life as an adventure, and for the unexpected and under-appreciated value of misadventure—for wrong turns and dead ends, chance discoveries and unintended turns. It makes life a matter of open-ended exploration instead of a predetermined slog along a straight line from birth to death.

Instead of what's *the* meaning of life, then, I'd rather ask what makes my life meaningful. Instead of mission, I'm happy to wake up in anticipation of a new day, with work I want to return to, people I want to walk and talk with. Happy, that is, to wake up with desire, with appetite, and with the bemused acceptance of being human, fallible, and imperfectly rational. I rejoice in there being no single meaning—in there being instead a multitude of meanings, an infinite number of ways in which we exercise our subjectivity and imagination, rendering meaningful what is objectively meaningless. Meaning is ours to make, and to choose.

The search for meaning, then, is itself a choice. It offers the hope of a consoling narrative that will stave off the awareness of an indifferent universe. It's the go-to defense against the fear of insignificance, against the realization that there's nothing personal in nature—that it's not about me, or you, or us—and that whatever narrative we detect in it is entirely of our own making. We make ourselves significant. We persuade ourselves that whales sing to us. Even, as happened to me, that a snow-covered mountain speaks to us.

MOUNT RAINIER RISES above the rest of the Cascade Range in solitary splendor. I think of it as the magic floating mountain, especially toward sunset, when it hovers ethereally on the horizon as in a Japanese brush painting of its trans-Pacific twin, Mount Fuji. At 14,411 feet, Rainier is the touchstone of the Seattle landscape, simultaneously familiar and remote. And deadly. More than four hundred climbers have died on this mountain since record-keeping began, because it creates its own weather. Even on otherwise clear days, there's often a lens-shaped cloud—a standing lenticular—hovering high above the peak. Such clouds look smooth and thus calm, but in fact they're formed by turbulence; what seems tranquil from sixty miles away may be anything but tranquil up close.

I'm no snow climber—Mount Sinai is a more natural habitat for me than Mount Rainier—so I'd chosen a clear summer day to hike several miles past the Carbon Glacier on the north slope of the mountain, up a series of steep switchbacks into a high valley of alpine flowers, where dozens of marmots had spread out on the sun-warmed rocks. At the head of the valley, the massive snow-covered peak beckoned, looking much closer than I knew it was. It took a while to register that as I'd walked on, the marmots had disappeared, and so had the sunshine. The single cloud I'd seen not long before had been swallowed up into a huge mass that obscured the peak and was expanding into a tumult of gray, then dark gray, then almost black. Even as I watched, this cloud mass was reaching down toward me, threatening to envelop me, and it was as though the mountain had its own will, one it was making known with an unmistakable message: "Get down off me now, because I can destroy you. I can make you disappear. I can show you my power, and you will never live to tell." What I felt then was not awe, but its awful shadow, dread.

Ridiculous, of course, to attribute intent to a mountain. I knew that it was only doing what such mountains do—making its own weather. There was no malevolence involved, no fatal intention, and no awareness on the mountain's part, only on mine. Yet something in me was convinced nonetheless that this was an intentionally ominous display of power.

Hard, heavy raindrops began to bounce off the rocks as I raced downward as fast I could. Each time I looked back, the mountain seemed more threatening, filling me with the visceral sense of an infinitely powerful presence—not of a divine being but of an implacable, unthinking, inhuman force that was very much of this world, in which my existence, this individual human life, was utterly irrelevant. Where I had climbed up as a nature romantic, I slipped and slid down as a drenched, shivering rat.

I may like to think that I have no illusions about the terms of my existence on this planet, but that itself is merely an illusion: my own pathetic fallacy. Romanticism lingers, a sop to my vanity, to my sense of the centrality of my own existence. However clearly I think I accept the ease with which I could, at any moment, cease to exist, some part of me stubbornly refuses to accept my own insignificance, and sees personal meaning in impersonal forces. I shamelessly insist, despite overwhelming evidence to the contrary, on my own significance.

SIX

THE SENSE OF AN ENDING

DEFINING THE MEANING OF LIFE IS

evidently an endless challenge. There are enough such definitions to fill a whole library, if not several of them. But this one, once read, is just about impossible to forget: "The meaning of life is that it stops."

I gave a small gasp when I first saw that sentence, as though a splash of cold water had just hit my brain. I love its sly wit: the promise of insight followed by that abruptly blunt conclusion. And it has the added advantage that it can be read several ways—as nihilistic pessimism, as mordant humor, as a sardonic take on promises of guru-like wisdom, or as a sharp dose of hard-nosed reality.

The quote is usually attributed to Kafka, though to my frustration, never with a precise citation. At one stage, I even contacted leading Kafka scholars in an effort to

track it down, but they replied that so far as they knew—
and they were pretty sure they knew every word he'd ever
written—it wasn't his. (I still haven't discovered the real
source, though Woody Allen might be a prime suspect.)
Nonetheless, I found myself repeating both the quote and
the attribution in an argument a couple of years back with
an enthusiastic proponent of the end-to-aging movement. The vision of a radically enhanced lifespan appears
to be especially beloved among Silicon Valley billionaires, many of whom are entranced by the potential of
biotechnology. One was actually boasting at the time that
he was taking 150 assorted nutritional supplements
daily—an activity that itself must have consumed the better part of an hour, let alone the lining of his stomach.
This did not seem to me a very good way of demonstrating
that long life was worth living.

The argument was at a cocktail party, which only
added to its Kafkaesque quality, since such parties are
not exactly where you expect to delve into existential
discussion. And the surrealism of our exchange was
exacerbated by the fact that my challenger was half my
age. Death was far more of an imminent reality for me

than for him, yet he seemed to take my equanimity at the prospect as an admission of some kind of failure. "How can you, of all people, accept limits that don't have to be there?" he asked. "Just think of everything you could achieve if you could double your lifespan."

I'm not sure if I laughed or winced. Probably both. "That seems kind of greedy," I said, only to set off an almost evangelical fervor as my new acquaintance did his best to convince me that advances in gene therapy and biomedical research could create not just an end to aging, but "an end to death." An end to death? I pointed out that this was surely the ultimate oxymoron, but to no effect, and took refuge in my drink. What he was advocating seemed an intensely depressing idea.

"But all this is tantamount to saying that science will cure life!" I finally countered. And then: "What's wrong with dying?"

The question startled him into silence. I was actually quite startled too. I'd never thought to ask that specific question before, never put it quite so baldly. But now that it was out there, hovering in the alcoholic fumes between us, it seemed to cut to the heart of the matter,

because of all the things-taken-for-granted, the fear of death has to be the largest.

We are, per any number of philosophers and psychologists whose work I otherwise respect, haunted by this fear. William James called death "the evil background" and "the worm at the core" of human aspirations to happiness. Poet Philip Larkin, who was very good at worms at the core of things (he famously described religion as "that vast, moth-eaten musical brocade") wrote of staying awake until dawn appalled at the prospect of his own death, "at the total emptiness for ever." Ernest Becker assumed the universality of such fear in his book *The Denial of Death*, which might be recommended as essential reading for tech billionaires, while fellow psychoanalyst Gregory Zilboorg went so far as to use this assumption as evidence, writing that "we may take it for granted that the fear of death is always present in our mental functioning." Since psychoanalysis is designed to probe beneath the taken-for-granted, the phrase "we may take it for granted" strikes me as an astonishing one for any of its practitioners to use. And as so often when something seems so obvious that it's beyond questioning, I'm not at all sure it's really so.

I HAVE BEEN close to my own death a number of times: shot at on assignment, bombed as a civilian, threatened by right-wing extremists as a journalist ("Let us know if they carry out the threats," said the police). But it was a relatively mundane car crash that felt the most immediate, perhaps because it was my own doing. I lost control of a car on a racetrack in the American Midwest, went into a long skid, and then, with what seemed immense slowness, rolled over. Several times. "This is it," I thought, with an oddly serene fatalism. "I'm going to die. Right here, right now. This is where my life flashes before me." Except it didn't. Despite reports of people seeing their lives unfurl before them in near-death experiences, I found myself stuck on one sentence, which reverberated over and over in my mind. "This," I kept thinking, "is a really stupid way to die."

The car came to a stop on what remained of its roof, with me hanging upside down in the seat harness. It took a few moments to register the mix of surprise and relief at finding myself bruised in body and ego but otherwise unhurt, thanks to my dented crash helmet. It occurred to me only later to wonder what would have made dying this way more stupid than, say, being killed in a war. And to ask exactly what I might consider an intelligent way to die.

To be embarrassed by the mode of one's own death is surely the epitome of egocentrism, let alone of absurdity. Despite myself, what I was really insisting on was that my death should have meaning, even though that meaning could have relevance only for me, and if I was dead, I'd no longer be around to appreciate it. I don't know if Thomas Nagel was ever in such a situation, but I'd later recognize my dilemma in what he wrote about dying: "From far enough outside"—his hypothetical "view from nowhere"—"my birth seems accidental, my life pointless, and my death insignificant. But from inside, my never having been born seems nearly unimaginable, my life monstrously important, and my death catastrophic."

That sounds right, and yet Nagel is being somewhat disingenuous here. Of course he can conceive of himself as not existing, or he would not have been able to write those sentences. It's the terms of his future non-existence that seem to be the problem, albeit an oxymoronic one, since non-existence can have no terms.

As many before Nagel have noted, the fact of our non-existence before we were born is not an issue, at least for those who do not believe in reincarnation. The world before me, that is, is not the world without me; but so far as I am concerned, the world after me most definitely is. My own future absence appears to be a humbling proposition. And an intensely personal one.

On the phylogenetic level—the terms of existence of the human race as a whole—massive threats such as nuclear war and global warming have raised the question of an end to the human race. One best-selling book, *The World Without Us*, explores how the natural world would reassert itself if all humans were to suddenly disappear in some absolute extinction (the answer: with amazing speed). But what we seem able to conceive of on a phylogenetic level becomes far more problematic on the ontogenetic one—the terms, that is, of your own individual existence. There appears to be a vast difference between imagining no human beings at all and imagining the absence of the one particular human being that is you.

Death can be seen as the ultimate threat to identity, the unavoidable insult to the sense of personal significance. Thus the pervasiveness of the question "What happens when I die?"—as though some part of us would still be alive to care. As though it were inconceivable that the world might exist without us.

RELIGION IS OFTEN at its best when dealing with death. Its rituals are designed to guide mourners through numbness and shock, and to give them a collective framework within which to actively grieve. The mourner's recitation of the Jewish kaddish prayer for the dead; the Islamic funeral chanting of the *fatiha*, the opening verses of the Quran; the three-day Hindu vigil over the body; the Celtic Catholic wake—all these are means of acknowledging and even honoring death. They work against denial.

Yet denial persists even within such traditions. "I wish you long life" is the standard way to greet a mourner in Judaism, for instance. The greeting is meant well, but I shuddered when it was said to me after my mother's death at age ninety, because I was not at all sure that long life was something devoutly to be wished. In fact she had assured me that it was not. Extended life can be a double-edged blessing—and possibly more curse than blessing. It prizes longevity over quality, the abstraction of numbers over the day-to-day reality of existence in a failing body.

How long a life do we really want? The average lifespan worldwide is now nearly twice what it was for most of history. To die of old age was once rare. It was only when the role of germs was recognized in the nineteenth century that wholesale death in epidemics began a rapid decline. Until antibiotics revolutionized twentieth-century medicine, something as minor as an infected tooth or an untreated cut could kill you, and death in childbirth or in infancy was common. Today's killer diseases—foremost among them cancer and heart disease—can be seen, with a certain stony irony, as the luxuries of Western modernity. They're the diseases you live long enough to die of.

So I have to concede that my cocktail-party challenger had an excellent point when he asked why I wouldn't want to double my lifespan. Since we've already done exactly that in the last century and a half, why not do it again if we can? After all, most Westerners are already living far beyond what nature alone would allow, as any person past middle age can attest on the most visceral level. Where most women once died before menopause, the vast majority now live through this unmistakable sign that there is no longer any biological "reason" for them to be alive. The commercial success of Viagra is an equally unmistakable sign of biological redundancy for men, as is the rapid decline of sperm count with age. Yet while the reproductive years are over, the productive ones are not, and the decades after menopause and its male equivalent are increasingly experienced not as a loss but as a gift. How big a gift should we demand, then? Is it churlish to ask for more, or only human? And what kind of "more" do we want?

Many people are now asking such questions, as was clear when physician Atul Gawande's *Being Mortal* became an instant bestseller. Doctors now have the ability to prolong life, or more precisely, to delay death. But when they act on it, many experience a kind of medical future shock, realizing with dismay that what they have really prolonged is suffering. Gawande was forthright about "the damage we in medicine do when we fail to acknowledge that the power to push against the constraints of biology is finite and always will be." What's feasible is not necessarily what's desirable.

By refusing to accept death—by seeing it as failure—both physicians and their patients act out the assumption that death is the enemy. When so many medical measures can be thrown at it, doing nothing can seem almost criminal. Every sane person wishes for a peaceful death, but that often involves the deliberate decision *not* to resuscitate, *not* to intervene except for palliative care, *not* to take every feasible measure. And the problem is right there in the phrasing. It's all in the negative instead of in the positive, can-do style so boosted in American society. Inaction is often seen as a kind of moral failure, even as an admission of defeat.

The language used for illness has thus become downright militaristic. If death is the enemy, it must be confronted with every available weapon in the medical arsenal. A kind of macho defiance is built into the idea of fighting off infection, battling cancer, or employing "heroic measures." And as though being ill were not hard enough, it is often transformed into a trial of moral and physical endurance, with the patient subjected to a boot-camp chorus of "You can do this, you can beat it." It's as though we've declared war on death. As though, absurdly, we could kill it.

IS "MAKING PEACE WITH DEATH" the alternative, then? Only if you accept the metaphor of making war on it to start with. True, there are times when I'm tempted to use the conventional RIP—"Rest in peace"—but that's when the lives of those who've died have been anything but peaceful. And even then, I am aware that I'm speaking to someone who is no longer there to hear me. What I'm really doing is telling myself to be at peace with their absence in my own life. Perhaps Shakespeare's Hamlet had it wrong and death doesn't make cowards of us all; it makes egocentrics of us all.

Still, there are times when the ego falls away and the prospect of one's own imminent death does seem seductively serene, and these are not necessarily times of depression or despair. Dehydration can have that effect, as I discovered the day I went bounding up a desert canyon far ahead of friends, indulging in the fantasy of myself as a mountain goat. Water? What mountain goat needs to drink water? Yet when I came to a large free-standing boulder blocking the way, the shade it cast looked so inviting that the mountain-goat image abruptly dissolved into that of a lizard. I crawled as far under the boulder as I could—the lizard in its lair—and closed my eyes in its dark shelter, thinking how pleasant it would be to take a very long nap. I was half-aware that this was dehydration talking, and that if I kept my eyes closed, I might very well never open them again, but this didn't seem a matter of great concern. Restful was the only word that made sense. When my friends caught up, I roused myself enough to tell them to go on ahead. "I'll catch up in a while," I said, slurring my words and knowing even as I spoke that this was a lie. It was my good fortune that they knew this too. They dragged me out despite my protests, poured their canteens over my head, and sip by sip, made me drink, sitting with me as my body temperature slowly returned to normal.

I suppose this might have been called a natural death if it had happened—death by nature, that is. Not out of a desire to die, but in a kind of surrender to it, without regret, without fear, without struggle or violence. Isn't this what we hope for ourselves, and for those we love?

But all, as it were, in good time. That spell of dehydration happened half my life ago, and I remain inordinately grateful to the friends who pulled me back. Yet I still do not fear the idea of my own death, despite the half-conscious temptation to cross my fingers as I say so.

This does not mean that I am reckless, desert and racetrack misadventures notwithstanding. I am terrified of many things that others undertake with relish, like strapping on a pair of skis or going underwater with a tank of oxygen on my back, neither of which will I ever bring myself to do. Nor does it mean that I am brave, since that would involve overcoming fear. It means that I neither embrace death nor fight it, but accept it as the necessary end to what I fully intend to be a well-lived life.

Do I leave myself open here to the charge of being in repression or denial? If you think so, let me ask another question instead: Are you really afraid of death? I've asked this of many people by now, and while most make it clear that they'd like to be able to die well—not stupidly, as in a rollover, and certainly not in helpless, protracted pain—the majority also say that no, they're not really that afraid of death itself. And they say this with evident surprise, as did neurologist Oliver Sacks when faced with terminal cancer. "I cannot pretend I am without fear," he wrote. "But my predominant feeling is one of gratitude. I have loved and been loved; I have been given much and I have given something in return; I have read and traveled and thought and written . . . Above all, I have been a sentient being, a thinking animal, on this beautiful planet, and that in itself has been an enormous privilege and adventure."

We've been told so often that everyone fears death that most of us no longer question whether this is really so. But when given the chance to step outside that assumption, it turns out that many, like Sacks, are less disturbed by an imminent ending than is generally supposed. I may not be that much of an outlier after all. In which case, it's worth asking what we're really afraid of. Might it be not death itself but quite the opposite? Rather than dying, might it be the thought of *not* dying, of living on in one form or another, that can be so intensely disturbing?

ENTER, THE AFTERLIFE. And with it, the imposition once again of the definite article, designed to endow its referent with the unassailable reality of well-charted territory, or at least to create room for a wary, Pascal-like "But what if they're right and there really is such a thing?"

"'Tis too horrible," declares Claudio in Shakespeare's *Measure for Measure*. "The weariest and most loathed worldly life / That age, ache, penury and imprisonment / Can lay on nature is a paradise / To what we fear of death." Or in the words given to Hamlet: "The dread of something after death . . . puzzles the will / And makes us rather bear the ills we have / Than fly to others that we know not of."

A prodigious amount of both poetic and religious energy has been devoted to the idea of life after death— the insistence that while your body may die, your soul, like John Brown's, goes marching on, and that what you do in this life determines your fate in the eternal next. This is, to put it mildly, a sobering thought to live with. But as with so much conservative religious doctrine, it may actually be a form of heresy. In the Bible itself, God does not take kindly to humans aiming for immortality. The divine judgment on Eve's bid for the fruit of the tree of knowledge is thus a multiple curse: not only a life of sweat and toil, and not only pain in childbirth, but also mortality, lest she and Adam "take also of the tree of life, and eat, and live for ever."

This astonishing judgment gets you both coming and going. Not only is life itself pronounced a curse—sweat, toil, and pain—but so too is death. One almost wants to respond that God should make up his mind. Yet the early Christian church had no such problems. By the second century, church fathers had seized on the idea of "original sin," and by the fifth, Augustine had elaborated it into what would become doctrine. To be human was to inherit the sin of Adam and Eve; it was to be born sinful. Only through obedience to the church could any human being hope for salvation—not in this life, but in a never-ending next one. God may have proclaimed that humans were mortal, but the church would now correct him, setting about the business of saving not bodies—they were evidently expendable—but souls.

In fairness, the idea of salvation may have originally been conceived of as a hopeful proposition, if in the dourest possible way. It made up for what was seen as the misery of this life by extending the carrot of eternal bliss in the next. If this life was a burden, the next one need not be; salvation offered a kind of divine atonement for inflicting the burden on you in the first place. But the carrot came with a stick, and what was offered as consolation was also inherently terrifying.

Being saved is based on fear, since you only need to be saved if you're under threat. The threat—damnation—would thus be elaborately laid out, embroidered into the tortures of hell and given vivid form in such works as Dante's *Inferno* and Hieronymus Bosch's paintings. The sword of eternal punishment hung over the heads of believers, cowing them into submission. Like repressive regimes everywhere, the medieval church would exert control through fear.

Death is indeed a terrifying prospect if what you face is even the possibility of eternal suffering. And although that amorphous carrot of heaven was on simultaneous offer, nobody knew better than the canny church fathers that saints are few and far between. In effect, the prospect of salvation was a form of life negation: not so much a denial of death as a denial of life. Whether you preened in righteous anticipation of the afterlife or more likely quivered in fear of it, the life you were actually living was rendered meaningless by comparison. It was a life endured under threat, with obedience imposed by a kind of theological Stockholm syndrome.

The many attempts to put an optimistic gloss on this somehow only end up making it worse. "Purpose driven" pastor Rick Warren, for instance, preaches that "you were put here to prepare for eternity" and that "earth is the staging area, the preschool, the tryout for your life in eternity." Really? Life as a practice session? How could anyone possibly take it seriously if so? Even as Warren claims to have the answer to the complex, fascinating, mysterious phenomenon of what we call existence, he pulls the rug out from under it by proclaiming it not the real thing.

And yet the Silicon Valley apostles of immortality do much the same, even if they think of eternal life as embodied rather than disembodied. Essentially, what they are advocating is a secular rebranding of the religious argument. Thus PayPal co-founder Peter Thiel's astonishing declaration that "if people think they are going to die, it is demotivating. The idea of immortality is motivational." The early church fathers could not have put it better.

As one of those people ridiculous enough to imagine that she's going to die, I have stared at Thiel's statement many times, and still find it hard to deal with its translation of existential questions into the language of corporate management. It implies that our lives are somehow invalidated by the fact that we will die, and assumes that life is a matter of metrics, its value determined by something as easily measurable as years. Along with other wealthy genomic dreamers, Thiel seems to think that what makes us get up in the morning and go to work is not the enjoyment of life expressed with such eloquence and grace by Oliver Sacks, but the hope and even the expectation that we will do so endlessly.

Whether motivated by simplistic religion or by biotech evangelism, the quest for immortality, whether in body or in soul, ignores an inherent paradox in how we think about our own existence. On the one hand, if we truly value life, we might fear death because it deprives us of more of the life we value; but on the other hand, we wouldn't be able to value life in the way we do if death never occurred. The awareness of mortality is part of what gives life meaning; it sharpens our appreciation of being alive, precisely because of the knowledge that we will not be alive forever. It's not mortality that drains life of meaning, but immortality.

Even as we might swear eternal love or loyalty, something in us is aware of how terrifyingly inhuman "forever" can be. The Greeks knew this. Immortality was the realm of the gods; they were known as the immortals, while the word mortal was a synonym for human (a usage that lasted well into the twentieth century). And since gods tend to be jealous, humans encroached on their realm only at great peril. Those who aspired to be as gods were punished with precisely what they sought: the inability to die. Thus Tantalus, surrounded by food and water yet forever unable to eat or drink. Or Sisyphus, eternally rolling his boulder uphill, indifferent to the defiant, almost desperate insistence of Albert Camus that "we must imagine Sisyphus happy."

The Bible may have declared mortality a curse, but the Greeks begged to differ. The real curse was immortality, and whatever church doctrine said, that realization found its way over the centuries into popular culture and folklore. Think of the anti-Semitic legend of the Wandering Jew, the cobbler who was accused of refusing Jesus permission to rest on his doorstep and was therefore sentenced to wander the world for eternity. Of Dracula the vampire, haunting others and yet haunted himself by his need for nightly blood. Of ghosts, condemned by misdeeds of the past to spectral half-lives in abandoned houses. Or even of a comic-book hero like Superman, destined never to have a regular Clark Kent life, never to live, love, and die like a normal human being.

We need endings. To live forever is the stuff of nightmares, and if we refuse to acknowledge this in principle, we at least do so in everyday speech. "It just went on and on," we might say of sitting through a boring lecture. "It was like it would never end." We complain of "incessant chatter," speak ironically of "deathless prose," describe a bad movie as "interminable." Consciously or not, we need the sense of narrative that comes with time. It's right there in the over-used metaphor of life as a journey—life as contained within time, that is, moving from beginning to end. As philosopher Samuel Scheffler put it in a Zen-like analogy, "A life without temporal boundaries would be no more a life than a circle without a circumference would be a circle."

The ability to die—our dieability, you might say—is an integral part of what makes us human. So while the early church authorities framed the expulsion from Eden as "the Fall" (a term that appears nowhere in the biblical account), it could with equal validity be framed as "the Rise." Until Eve takes that bite of the apple, she and Adam may have human form, but they don't have human minds. They're more like well-trained pets, given free range except for the two forbidden trees. The moment they taste the fruit of the tree of knowledge is the moment they achieve both consciousness and its correlate, self-consciousness. This is where they step into awareness of their own existence. The expulsion from the tame, unthinking existence of Eden can thus equally be seen as the liberation from it. The first couple were now free to be fully human and thus mortal, capable of experiencing what ethicist Hans Jonas movingly called "the pang and poignancy of finitude."

Without that pang and poignancy—without the awareness of death—life would become a flat, featureless expanse, just-one-thing-after-another literally ad infinitum. A narrative void, it would suck the vitality out of existence and eviscerate it of meaning, of the multiple, individual ways of understanding ourselves in the world. Indeed this is one way of describing the sense of tedium and pointlessness that typifies chronic depression. And yet it seems to be precisely those who derive the least pleasure from life who most fear its cessation. They favor the Germanic gloom of philosopher Arthur Schopenhauer, who maintained that "the love of life is at bottom only the fear of death." Which doesn't sound at all like love to me. This does: "The fear of death follows from the fear of life." That's Mark Twain, and at the risk of forfeiting my intellectual chops, I'll go with the sage of the Mississippi over the perpetually dissatisfied metaphysicist anytime.

For myself, I have no intention of only half-living this life in anticipation of a hypothetical next one. I want to live my life as well and as fully as I can—in consciousness, in commitment, in full acknowledgment of its difficulties as well as its occasional rewards, its pains as well as its pleasures, its absurdities as well as its mysteries. The last thing I would ever want is to have no end, to find myself adrift in the horizonless expanse of eternity. I want, that is, to live the mortal life I have.

SEVEN

EVERY THING
AND MORE

AT NINE YEARS OLD, I'D LIE ON THE
living-room floor trying again and again to write my
address in a school notebook. My full address, that is—
the fullest one possible. Much later, I found out that
Picasso had used a similar notebook in France, its plain
brown cover printed simply with the title *Cahier*. In
the space allotted for ownership, he wrote "Monsieur
Picasso, peintre, 13 Rue Ravignan, Paris XVIIIᵉ," and
then added three words above the title to create a defiant
declaration: *Je suis le Cahier.* I wish I'd had that elegance
of wit, but at nine, I was not nearly as sure of my place in
the world as Picasso had been; few people ever are. And
besides, I was determined to be literal.

The first few lines of my address were easy enough:
street, neighborhood, city, country—the familiar post
office format. But I became less confident as I stepped

up to continent, planet, solar system, galaxy . . . and then what? That childish "and then" was a challenge to think further, to keep going one more line, one conceptual level larger. But if my mind was up to the challenge, my knowledge was not. Finally, for lack of an alternative, I'd write "The Universe" and draw a neat line under it. Too neat. It felt peculiarly unsatisfactory—a kind of shorthand for what I sensed might be, but had no way of grasping. Despite the assertion of its uppercase letters, "The Universe" was less a location than a generalization, a symbolic way of saying "everything and more," which is how the writer David Foster Wallace would title his book on infinity. I can think of no better definition.

At the time, I didn't even know such a concept existed. Sure, the nuns at the convent school I attended talked of God's infinite goodness and wisdom, but that seemed just a turn of phrase, a slice of piety to be taken no more seriously than a "bless you" when someone sneezed. I had no idea that mathematicians had already refined infinite smallness—the infinitesimal—into the basis of quantum theory, and no way of knowing that I was not the only person puzzling at the trans-finite, or just how large largeness can be.

We count, and by counting, assign an order to things. This is what I kept trying to do on the living-room floor, where I'd give up on my address and start working my way through the atlas, page by page, counting seas. I'm not sure why seas exactly, as opposed to mountains or deserts; my only experience of the sea at that age was the pebbled chilliness of the English coastline. Perhaps I was just struck by the evident wrongness of the old expression "the seven seas," and thought that if I could come up with a definitive count, I'd understand something more about the world. Each time I tried, however, I'd arrive at a different number, and so had to start again.

It didn't occur to me then that seas could not be contained in numbers. Or that numbers themselves might not be containable. Or that my attempt to understand my place on the planet and in the universe might be an attempt to defeat infinity, or at least deconstruct it.

The basis of infinity is deceptively simple: there is no end to numbers. However large a number you can come up with, you can always add 1. Simple, but frustrating. For a number-counting species such as ours, the prospect of numbers without end can seem terrifyingly anarchic. Yet being contradictory creatures, we speak with cavalier ease of things being countless. We've all done it countless times. Some of those times, it's because we can't be bothered to count; others, it's more of an evasion, even a denial of what countlessness really means.

One of the great conundrums of human consciousness is that we can conceive of things that, strictly speaking, we can't conceive of. We conceive, that is, of the inconceivable, and this is what makes infinity so ineffably daunting. Infinity *is* the view from nowhere. It challenges not only what we think of as common sense, but also our whole concept of the world. It makes nonsense of both egocentrism and anthropocentrism—in fact, of all kinds of centrism. And since it is immeasurably larger and grander than the anthropomorphic divinity of biblical renown, infinity may in fact be closer to how most people really think of God than anything theology has yet conceived of.

The mathematical symbol for infinity—∞—is known as the lemniscate, from the Greek for ribbon, since it winds in on itself, doubling the ancient archetype of the ouroboros, a snake curled into a circle with its tail in its mouth. The ouroboros signifies eternal renewal, and if that word eternal sounds somewhat outdated, a religious term floating in a kind of poetic haze, you could say that the mathematical investigation of infinity is what makes eternity scientifically respectable. Formulaic expressions such as "world without end" and "forever and ever" come alive when seen through the lens of pure reason, and even achieve a transcendent precision. Here, at the outer limits of mathematics, the mind soars and numbers shimmer, as though the ancient idea of *musica universalis*, the harmony of the spheres, were almost, tantalizingly, within reach.

Too poetic? Consider what David Hilbert, one of the most influential mathematicians of the twentieth century, said when he heard that one of his students had dropped out to write poetry: "Good—he didn't have enough imagination to become a mathematician." Or the fact that when Hilbert first began to publish his work on finiteness and infinity, one leading critic maintained, "This is not mathematics; this is theology." The critic later backtracked ("I have convinced myself that even theology has its merits"), but since infinity abounds with paradox, he could also be said to have had an excellent point. As experts in infinity, mathematicians could be thought of as the theologists of the twenty-first century.

MOST OF US are no good at thinking about immensity, let alone infinity. We read about billions and trillions of miles in space and our minds either reel or go numb. Dealing with such numbers is heady business because the head is where they exist. They seem solid, but that's an illusion. In a sense, all numbers are imaginary, and mathematical terminology acknowledges this. There are rational and irrational numbers; amicable and sociable numbers; weird and narcissistic numbers; and perhaps most seductively of all for the theologically inclined, transcendental numbers, which do indeed transcend mathematical analysis, which is why they've been called the dark matter of the number universe. The best-known transcendentals, π and e (the constant of exponential growth), seem to have a kind of autonomous existence, an insistent reality beyond abstraction.

It's only when we have concrete images that we begin to appreciate the dimensions of immensity. If you're thirty-one years old, for instance, you will live the billionth second of your life this year. That's a little mind-blow right there. But what then of a number that dwarfs a mere billion, like a googol? This is mathematical shorthand for one to the power of ten, or the number 1 followed by a hundred zeroes. The name was coined by another nine-year-old, the nephew of the mathematician who came up with it in 1937, leading to its adoption sixty years later—unintentionally misspelled, as legend has it—by the founders of Google.

A googol is indeed large, but it's still graspable; if you are suitably obsessive, you can write it out in a couple of lines. So it was quickly outsized by the googolplex, which the same young nephew defined as "one followed by writing zeroes until you get tired." His uncle, aiming for somewhat more precision, made it ten to the power of a googol, or the number 1 followed by a googol zeroes. I'd say write that out, except that no matter how obsessive you may be, you can't. Even if you could write a zero on every single atom in the universe, there's not enough room to write all the zeroes of a googolplex.

And that's not the biggest number there is. Since the logic of numbers means that big can always be bigger, the googolplex would in turn be superseded by entities like Graham's number, named for the man who first posited it. This is to a googolplex as a googolplex is to the number 10, and I would say that this is inconceivably large, except of course for the fact that Ronald Graham conceived of it. But forget even thinking about writing out Graham's number, because it's inexpressible. Mathematicians know it exists, but it defies any attempt to represent it either in conventional numerical terms or in terms of something we can more or less understand, like the number of atoms in the universe. Yet even such an indeterminable number is ultimately finite. However large it may be, it might as well be zero compared with infinity. As Graham himself put it, "Infinity is just out there. It's a different beast." And wrestling with the beast can be a delight or a nightmare.

THE DELIGHT IS on abundant display at the Numberphile channel on YouTube, where rumpled young academics from the Mathematical Sciences Research Institute brim with infectious enthusiasm (a word that comes from the Greek *en-theos*, god-filled) as they scrawl out their equations on sheets of butcher paper. My favorite, and one of the most hotly debated, features physicist and Royal Society fellow Tony Padilla, who shows that when you add all the whole positive numbers from 1 to infinity, the result is $-\frac{1}{12}$. (That is not a typo. It really is minus one-twelfth. And while there are many technical proofs of this, Padilla does it in a way that even I can almost follow.) "That's amazing—I love it!" he declares with a huge grin as he sits back and contemplates his work. Asked what would happen if he were to add all the whole numbers from 1 to a googolplex, he answers with deadpan straight-forwardness: "You'd get a very big number. You wouldn't get $-\frac{1}{12}$. To get $-\frac{1}{12}$, you have to go to infinity."

To say that this result is counter-intuitive is a glaring understatement. "It can't be," is the usual reaction. We think of the cool logic of mathematical analysis as the highest form of reason, yet in such instances, it defies everything we think of as reason. This is what infinity does. It teems with paradox and conundrum. It soars beyond conventional ideas of rational and irrational, leaving you either gaping in awe or laughing helplessly at everything you thought you knew. And that's just the beginning, as it were. Logic turns from cool to white-hot—indeed for some, it becomes a black hole—when you come up against the idea that there is no single infinity. Instead, there are infinities within infinities.

This is not some kind of mystical mantra. Some infinities actually are larger than others, and it's provable. On the simplest level, for example, imagine making two lists of numbers: the first contains all whole numbers to infinity, and the second, only odd numbers to infinity. Since the second list has half as many numbers as the first, it seems only reasonable to assume that it will be half as long, yet the two lists will in principle turn out to be the same size, because they both go on forever. A far more intricate example was dreamed up by David Hilbert, who dubbed it the paradox of the Grand Hotel. This imaginary hotel has an infinite number of rooms and is always fully occupied. Yet a mathematically minded manager can always figure out how to accommodate busloads of last-minute arrivals—even an infinite number of busloads, and even when each bus has an infinite number of seats. Infinity, that is, can absorb any number of other infinities, including an infinite number of them. There is always room for more.

If this seems like mere gamesmanship, the kind of head-spinning logic designed to stump you in quizzes, the fact is that it works in the real, earthbound world. On the quantum level—the infinitesimal, that is—physicists find that mysterious sums such as $-\frac{1}{12}$ are quite common. And what appear to be "vertiginous levels of abstraction," as David Foster Wallace put it, turn out to have extraordinary practical applications. Among other things, they've enabled the whole field of information and communications technology. But turn from the infinitely small to the infinitely large—to the trans-finite level of the cosmic—and the prospect can be so daunting that one elder statesman of mathematics was driven to declare, "I prefer a finite universe because I can get my mind around that. An infinite universe makes no sense to me." Even Einstein is said to have resisted the idea.

There's a certain comfort in the illusion that we can get our minds around things, as though we could pin them down and think no further. But "further" is where thought leads, out to the edge of what seems reasonable, and then beyond. So while some may see the idea of infinity as an insult to common sense, others see it as a magnificent challenge, an open invitation to transcend accepted limits of human thought. And in the process, they're raising serious questions about the very concept of the universe, since that term implies a single, bounded whole—one that may well be of our own imagining.

NUMBERS MAKE THE UNIVERSE reassuringly comprehensible, or at least they seem to. We know, for instance, that light travels at about 186,000 miles per second, which is 671 million miles per hour, or almost 6 trillion miles per year (a.k.a. a light-year). This means that when you look up into the sky, what you see is old light. You're looking out into space, and back in time. You see the moon as it was 1.282 seconds ago, the sun as it was 8.3 minutes ago, and the furthest galaxy yet detected by the Hubble Space Telescope (a reddish blob dubbed UDFj-39546284 and clearly in need of a nine-year-old to name it) as it was just over 13 billion years ago.

Yet despite the apparent precision of such numbers, there's a sense in which we're still living in the time of Copernicus. Our understanding has expanded exponentially since he established that the earth was not the center of the world, but geocentrism still exerts a pull on our minds as strong as that of gravity on our bodies. We tend to think of the universe as a singular entity, as though what we can observe—the spherical region of space from which light has had time to reach us since the big bang—is all there is. And we talk of the big bang as if it were the only one that ever took place, when it seems entirely probable that this was really *our* big bang—just one of an infinite number continuing through both space and time. Indeed, as MIT cosmologist Max Tegmark points out, "We don't even know for sure that our universe really had a beginning at all, as opposed to spending an eternity doing something we don't understand prior to the big bang nucleosynthesis."

It's often said that the more we know, the more we know we don't know—the kind of remark that gets people nodding sagaciously only to begin their response with "But . . ." Even as we acknowledge this in principle, we hanker for the security of convincing ourselves that we understand reality, and that everything can be neatly laid out in a self-contained system. Both bad science and bad religion operate on this assumption. Thomas Kuhn's view of scientific thought as an evolving series of paradigms may have become a staple of Science 101—a paradigm in itself—but the seduction of certainty still leads us to think of our current paradigms as unassailable fact.

The best scientists, however, like the best theologists, are under no such illusion of omniscience. Quantum theorists freely acknowledge how strange it is to work with mathematical concepts that have no physical correlates and seem to defy reason. "Quantum weirdness," they call it. And it's precisely this weirdness that impels them to explore further, to push the boundaries of the intellectual envelope in which we are tempted to seal ourselves.

Infinity exposes the pathos of the illusion of knowing. In what might be the ultimate pathetic fallacy, we search for "intelligent life in the universe" by sending out space capsules marked with mathematical symbols and Leonardo-like drawings of a man and a woman, on the assumption that any intelligent life elsewhere will be able to decipher them. We think of such possible intelligence, that is, as somehow resembling our own, because we cannot conceive of any other kind. Even as we probe the unknown, we are hampered by the known. As Tegmark notes, "Because we observe space to have the same properties everywhere in our universe, we're tempted to mistakenly conclude that space is like that everywhere else as well."

Tegmark is one of many physicists now making the argument that there are multiple universes in the cosmos, a literally countless number of them, which may or may not operate according to what we have determined to be the laws of physics applicable in our own. Life in these other universes may well take forms beyond human imagination, beyond even the magnificently impervious black stone slab in Stanley Kubrick's classic movie *2001: A Space Odyssey*. So while most of us still speak of "life" as though it were necessarily life as we know it, scientists now use the more accurate term "carbon-based life-forms," which allows (at least in principle, and without getting all sci-fi about it) the possibility of the existence of other life-forms in other regions of a universe, or multiverse, of which ours is only an infinitesimally small part.

Some people find this expanded sense of perspective liberating. Others find it intensely sobering and even maddening: With so much possibility, what certainties are left to hang on to? What comfort is there to be had?

Like Kubrick's stone slab, infinity challenges what we think we know. It makes no demand of belief. It simply is. Or could be. Or has to be. Thinking about it becomes something like playing a chess game on a board that doesn't actually exist, or rather, that exists beyond what we refer to as physical reality—another form of reality so removed from human sensory experience that it really can drive you out of your mind.

That's what happened to Georg Cantor, the inventor of mathematical set theory, whose work first implied "an infinity of infinities" and who spent the last thirty years of his life in and out of psychiatric hospitals. As though acknowledging that infinity is where the boundaries dissolve between reason and unreason, science and mysticism, Cantor blended mathematical and religious symbolism. Introducing the notation still used for infinite sets, he adopted the Hebrew letter ℵ and the Greek Ω, thus mirroring "the alpha and omega, the first and the last, the beginning and the end" in the book of Revelation. His successor David Hilbert picked up on the biblical metaphor, declaring that "nobody shall expel us from the Paradise that Cantor has created."

Paradise? Revelation? Perhaps it's inevitable: mathematical language demands huge expertise, while religious language is readily available. Infinity is where physics veers into metaphysics, where mathematics becomes mystery. As I grappled with the logic of it, I found myself thinking of the kabbalistic concept of the *Ein Sof*, the "no end." I went back to T. S. Eliot's "East Coker," which is shot through with Hindu mysticism, opening with "In my beginning is my end" and concluding with "In my end is my beginning." And as I watched those enthused research mathematicians on YouTube, the phrase that came to mind was "at play in the fields of the Lord," the title adapted by Peter Matthiessen from the ecstatic naturalism expressed by John Muir when he called Yosemite a place of "endless Godful play." Being a literary creature, I looked to words to express what exceeds words.

Even the most secular mind tends to fall back on the familiar narrative of religion as a way of containing the uncontainable, conceiving of the inconceivable. Or maybe not quite so familiar. Just as the baffling precision of infinity takes us beyond the vagueness of eternity, so science can take us beyond simplistic religion to something far closer to the essence of religious experience.

Einstein wrote of "this huge world out yonder which exists independently of us human beings, and which stands before us like a great, eternal riddle, at least partially accessible to our inspection and thinking." When asked if he thought of this "great, eternal riddle" as God, he replied, "The religious feeling engendered by experiencing the logical comprehensibility of profound interrelations is of a somewhat different sort than the feeling one usually calls religious. It is more of a feeling of awe at the scheme that is manifested in the material universe. It does not lead us to the step of fashioning a god-like being in our own image—a personage who makes demands of us and who takes an interest is us as individuals." And in conscious echo of Spinoza's dictum that "God is being itself, not *a* being," he concluded, "There is neither a will nor a goal, nor a must, but only sheer being."

LET ME BRING this back down to earth, or at least pretty close to earth, as I do when I head for the mountains, drawn as always to high places. There, on a clear moonless night, far away from artificial light, I can see the Milky Way. I can stretch my arms out wide and indulge in the illusion that I am holding the huge arc of it as it pours from one upturned palm into the other. Standing with this span of stars balanced in my hands, I seem to encompass infinite space.

I know that the Milky Way is not infinite; it's about a hundred thousand light years in diameter, or roughly 600,000 trillion miles. And I know too that what I imagine I am balancing from palm to palm is not even the whole of our galaxy but merely the outer edge of one of its many spirals, and that this galaxy is itself only one of billions of galaxies that we know of and a potentially infinite number that we don't know of. Yet this knowledge in no way detracts from the transcendent feeling of the moment. On the contrary, it expands it. Whether in the Cascades or the Sinai, I stand under a sky so dense with pinpoints of light that the old phrase "a canopy of stars" seems the only one that will do. Feeling both infinitesimally small and yet at the same time—absurdly, elatedly—at home in the universe, I revel in the sense of being, as the mystics would say, at one with the world.

To be both large and small—that's where physics is now, arcing between the general relativity theory of the large and the quantum physics of the small. On the one hand, a continuum of space-time, and on the other, an infinitely divisible reality in which physical existence is a matter not of certainties but of probabilities. And on a personal level, this is also how most of us now live.

Our lives are larger—it's tempting to say infinitely larger—than they were just a hundred or even fifty years ago. We can view photographs of spectacular nebulae taken from space probes yet remain as personally involved as ever with one another in everyday life, in the many forms of love, friendship, neighborliness, collegiality, community. Defying our own limits, we live big and small at the same time, with minds capable of focusing on both the cosmic and the mundane. We exist as finite beings within infinity, and if we are alive to this, it sharpens our delight in the mysterious fact of our existence.

The awareness of infinity is inexorably paradoxical, and this is what I love about it. It takes me out of myself and yet grounds me solidly at the same time, creating an awesomely inhuman perspective even as I remain mired in the day-to-day business of being human. And it allows me to take nothing for granted. What stumped me as a child at the start of the nuclear age now stuns me as an adult trying to work my mind around the weirdness of modern physics. Would the nine-year-old me have been able to complete her address with the word infinity and sit back with satisfaction? I doubt it. The glory of the concept of infinity is that it always has room for more. It is an endless, open invitation to live larger.

I have no conclusion here (how could I, when the subject is infinity?), except to say that to my agnostic eye, that mountaintop sense of being at home in the universe—that ephemeral yet deep sense of connection—may be the essence of real religious feeling. Not paradise, that is, nor revelation, nor even a minor epiphany, but something more modest and I hope more familiar: a simple gratefulness at being able to stand beneath the Milky Way in amazement and perplexity, fully conscious of the plain yet infinitely complex fact of my own stubborn, undeniable, improbable vitality.

EIGHT | IMPERFECT SOUL

SOMETIMES A STORY IS NOT BE-

lievable, but is deeply satisfying nonetheless. Perhaps all the best stories are like this, in which case one of them is surely the kabbalist legend of "the shattering of the vessels," where the world began, at least in my re-telling of it, with a kind of divine "Oops!"

The story comes from the teachings of Isaac Luria, the sixteenth-century mystic widely considered the father of kabbala. In it, the *Ein Sof*—the Endless—"contracted itself" to make room for the world, and as it did so, its light poured into ten vessels. Why ten is unclear, as is what exactly they were. What does seem clear, however, is that they were peculiarly fragile. Seven of them shattered and splintered into shards, which then fell into the abyss of *tohu ve'bohu*, the primordial chaos and darkness. But sparks of the divine light still clung to the shards as they fell, so the kabbalist task is to raise these sparks up out of the darkness in the process known as *tikkun olam*, or repairing the world, thus paving the way for the coming of the messiah.

Messianic chronologies are always strange, but this has to be one of the strangest, since it means that the world needs to be perfect in order to be made perfect. Or as Kafka tartly put it, "The messiah will come only when he is no longer needed." But then the whole story is peculiar. How did those vessels shatter in the first place? Was the beginning of the world as we know it just an accident? A cosmic mistake? A divine one? Even as it tries to avoid anthropomorphism, the story invites it. I imagine a Michelangeloid God walking along while trying to keep hold of ten vessels at once, much as you or I might foolishly try to hold ten bottles of wine. And then? How utterly human that he'd trip, stumble, and lose his grip in that divine Oops.

Each person reads such a story through their own lens. For Gershom Scholem, the great scholar of kabbalist philosophy, it was an image of exile—a metaphor of divine withdrawal from the world. "The historical notion of exile," he wrote, "had become a cosmic symbol."

Perhaps it was only natural that he'd see it this way, being an exile from Germany living in Israel, a country founded by exiles to end exile. But for twenty-first-century global nomads—people like myself who have lived in more than one place, and in my case on three continents—exile may be more a matter of choice than of dispossession. They might see the story instead as a kind of mystical chaos theory: a search for order within what appears to be infinite disorder. Or, as I see it, a story about fallibility, and thus an unruly, even outrageous, challenge to received theologies insisting on perfection.

"Be ye therefore perfect, even as your father which is in heaven is perfect," says Jesus in the Gospel of Matthew. Pious Muslims insist that Muhammad was the perfect man, and while Saint Augustine would assert that only God is perfect, he also allowed that human perfection might be attainable by divine grace. Yet tradition has rarely been so sure. Orthodox Jews still leave a small patch of wall unpainted as a safeguard against the hubris of aspiring to divine perfection, while Muslim artisans deliberately weave inconspicuous mistakes into a carpet, as though in acknowledgment of the ancient Latin adage *Errare humanum est*, "To err is human."

(It wasn't until the year 1711 that Alexander Pope added "to forgive, divine.")

But when it's not only humans, but God that's fallible? The shattering of the vessels posits a clumsy creator, a fallible god as a means of explaining a demonstrably fallible world. What a challenging proposition! And yet what a reassuring one also: a counterpart to the hubristic idea of perfectibility. If the Ein Sof is imperfect, maybe we humans can give ourselves permission to be imperfect too.

Perfection may be an ideal, but whether it's a desirable one is another question. Ideals are by definition products of the imagination rather than of reality; they exist, that is, as ideas, not as facts. The perfect truths of theology, claimed as "absolute truths," are thus inherently self-contradictory, because as William James noted, truth is always an evolving idea. "It is temporary, and constructed from our own experience . . ." he wrote. "The 'absolutely' true, meaning what no farther experience will ever alter, is that ideal vanishing-point towards which we imagine all our temporary truths will some day converge." It is, in short, imaginary.

A hundred years later, this is not exactly a popular

idea. Perfection is on offer all around us. Every student who takes a multiple-choice exam is suckered into the assumption that a 100 percent score indicates perfect knowledge; anyone who watches television takes in a steady diet of ads promoting the perfect product; every person tempted by cosmetic surgery subscribes to the artifice of perfectibility. Little more than a century after Nietzsche introduced the idea of the Übermensch, genetic engineers now have the controversial ability to edit DNA and insert their ideas of beauty and intelligence into the human genome. For the first time in human history, we live with the idea that perfection is attainable, not in a hypothetical next world but in this one.

But what would perfection consist of? The lion lying down with the lamb? Wonderful for the lamb, perhaps, but the lion would starve. The "more perfect Union" of the Constitution of the United States is evocative precisely in its elusiveness, let alone its grammatical impossibility. And while the biblical Eden is presented as a perfect place, the first humans' existence in it can well be seen as a life of mindless boredom, even as an early version of Aldous Huxley's *Brave New World*.

There's an icy starkness to perfection, a kind of

echoing emptiness. Perfection, that is, is soulless. And lifeless. Its real meaning is right there in its origin: the Latin *perficere*, to finish or to conclude. A perfect life would thus be one that is completed, and there is only one way that can happen. Perfection is literally a dead end. And to be alive is necessarily to be incomplete and thus imperfect, each person in his or her own particular way.

This is why the idea of perfectibility seems so hollow to me. The definitiveness, the absolutism, the dead-endness of it—all these leave no room for life. The perfect tomato in the store turns out to be tasteless, genetically engineered for shelf appeal, not for the palette. A flaw-less face seems blankly unapproachable, leaving me unable to do anything but puzzle at its unnatural symmetry. Complete agreement with whatever I might say leaves me gasping for intellectual air, longing for something more than a mirror of my own thoughts.

Or take what happened when a tiny Tokyo sushi bar was given the highest Michelin rating and its chef starred in the documentary *Jiro Dreams of Sushi*. Gour-mets from around the world rushed to eat there, eager to experience what was said to be perfection. My own response was quite the opposite, but not because I don't like sushi. Indeed I love it, and would happily dine out on it every night. But the last place I'd want to go would be Jiro's. Because let's assume for a moment that all those jet-setting gourmets are right—that there is such a thing as perfect sushi, and that Jiro's is it. What then? Once you've tasted perfection, what's left? No other sushi will ever again be as good; it will always suffer by comparison. The perfect sushi, that is, would result in a lifetime of disappointment. It would, in effect, be an end to all sushi. So instead of leaving me in a state of utopian longing, Jiro's obsessive perfectionism struck me as soulless, even robotic. And it seemed to run counter to one of Japan's best-known spiritual traditions.

The great Zen Buddhist masters knew what those who seek perfection do not: it leaves us cold. A classic Zen exercise is the *ensō*, the circle hand-drawn in a single fluid brushstroke. It is close to perfect, but never there. If perfection is what you want, you can produce it anytime by using a compass or a computer, but the *ensō* defies such mechanistic precision; indeed it is often incomplete, left slightly open as though in invitation to everything beyond it. And each one is different, never the same circle twice. You can see the hairs of the brush in the drag of the ink on the paper; trace the fluidity of the moment when the stillness of meditation was released in one rapid stroke; sense the calm grace of the artist. The beauty of the Zen circle lies precisely (or more precisely, imprecisely) in its imperfection. That is what speaks to us, and draws us in. A perfect circle is uninteresting, a closed system containing nothing, while an imperfect one vibrates with warmth. It invites us into the moment of its creation, into that single deep exhalation as the hand arced through the air, the brush over the paper. It is open, human, fallible—an expression, that is, of soul.

PERHAPS YOU HAVE to be slightly crazy to even try to talk about soul in secular terms. The more you try—the more I try, in any case—the greater the risk of falling into cliché, into the trite generalizations and warm fuzziness too often mistaken for spiritual insight. There's an easy sentimentality to the idea of someone being soulful, for example, or in the way my Irish mother used to make kind excuses for a rather tiresome acquaintance by saying, "Ah, but she's a good soul." There's the danger, that is, of entering chicken-soup-for-the-soul territory.

A strong whiff of sanctimony hovers over the word, burdened as it has been with such modifiers as blessed and immortal. That tyranny of the definite article—*the* soul—reasserts itself with implacable conviction, and conventional theology again becomes more hindrance than help. You'd think, since we use the word soul so much, we'd have a language for it. But we really don't. For all the talk of soul music, soul food, soul mates, soul sisters and brothers, of someone being soulful or soulless, of good souls, wretched souls, lost souls, fortunate souls, souls of discretion or brevity or kindness, we seem to end up in a haze of well-meaning sentiment. Soul, that is, is a soft concept. Be hard-headed about soul? You might as well try to be hard-headed about puppies.

Yet I persist, because I sense—and sense is the only word I can use here—that it's important to reclaim soul from those who still conceive of it as a thing with an immortal life of its own, independent of the body. However vague we may be about it, I think most of us recognize soul not as a thing, but as a dimension of being that defies the narrow lens of dogma, going far beyond traditional religious ideas such as those I grew up with.

I'm not sure how old I was when I first heard talk of

the soul (I'd be tempted to call it soul talk if there hadn't been something distinctly soulless about it), but in the convent school, it must have been quite early. None of the nuns ever explained exactly what a soul was, though they prayed a lot for lost ones, and I was given to understand that I might be one of those who had been so careless as to lose hers. The fact that I didn't know what it was only seemed proof of this. The best I could come up with was something like Peter Pan's shadow, which caused him such distress when it was snapped off, and such relief when Wendy sewed it back on. To lose your shadow was clearly a terrible thing, and for a while, I did much looking behind me to make sure mine was still there. Carl Jung, with his theory of the unconscious as "the shadow aspect," would have loved me.

I soon graduated to testing my shadow, seeing if I could confuse it and shake it off by spinning around. But although it kept shifting shape, it stayed stubbornly attached to me. This shadow was mine and yet not mine, visible and yet intangible, real and yet not-real. It would be oddly satisfying when I later discovered that ghosts were once called shades, and that vampires are said to cast no shadows, despite the magnificent use of them in the earliest of all vampire movies, F. W. Murnau's *Nosferatu*. At least I could see my shadow, if only on beclouded England's summer days. But my soul, to the extent that it was allowed that I still might have one, remained frustratingly elusive.

Others, however, evidently considered the soul to be something very concrete. Descartes, for instance, confidently asserted that it was located in the pineal gland, which is still thought of in spiritualist circles as the home of the supposed "third eye." One early-twentieth-century Massachusetts country doctor even claimed to have measured the weight of the soul as it left the body at death, concluding that it was three-quarters of an ounce. (Undeterred by actual science, popular legend would adopt his finding, converting it into twenty-one grams and thus giving Mexican director Alejandro González Iñárritu the title for one of his best films.) But a hundred years ago, it was easy to think of the soul as having a physical existence, since that was how people still spoke. Souls *were* people. "There wasn't a soul in sight," someone might say of an empty street, or, "All souls were lost at sea." The usage reflected the long arm of religious doctrine, less concerned with the mortal than with the immortal. By privileging existence in a hypothetical next world to life in this one, it succumbed, as militant fundamentalists still do, to the obscene idea that bodies were expendable, and that a life lost could be a soul found.

But what if we were to reclaim soul from the lost-and-found business? After all, it hasn't always been the exclusive province of religion. Back when the wealthy still ate goose for supper, the bird's lungs were called the soul and considered the finest delicacy. More ominously, the bore of a cannon was given the same name. The word is still used with far greater resonance for a violin's sound post—the peg beneath the bridge, which transmits and distributes the vibration of the instrument, giving it unique tone and depth. The soul is what enables the violin to resonate, to reach out into the world.

Why not reach out further, though, and abandon the "the" altogether? Instead of thinking of soul as some hidden interior component, what if we were to think of it instead as a mode of being in and with the world? Soul, that is, not as a possession—not as a part of you that lives on after death, or that can be lost like Peter Pan's shadow, or found and weighed whether in church or in the lab—but as a quality of existence. What might happen if we were to open out the idea and . . . well, give it soul again?

I MAY WELL BE on a fool's errand here. Approach the sense of soul directly, and it proves evanescent. Like time, it slips through your fingers. Ask what's meant by saying that someone's got soul, and you find yourself faced with a standard checklist of qualities such as generosity, warmth, openness, humility, genuineness, empathy. In short, well-meaning generalities. Vital as such qualities most certainly are, vitality is exactly what they seem to lack when listed this way, as though weighed down by earnest gravity. This may be why a sense of humor is conspicuous in its absence from the list. There is, as the kabbalist Luria might have said, no spark.

Better a fool for trying, however, than another kind of fool for not trying. But perhaps not head-on. An indirect approach might offer at least a glimpse of what we really mean by soul. And not only in a person. Every so often, for instance, I come across what is intended to be a provocative headline to an article about a city or a neighborhood, even a country: "Has [your city here] lost its soul?" It's a rhetorical question, of course, since the assumption is that if you have to ask, the answer is yes. But it does address something important, and that's the "feel" of a place: the ornery mix of qualities that make it unique, make it feel like home. This can't be measured by the usual quality-of-life factors such as transportation, services, and convenience. The question speaks instead to something that defies measurement, to the sense of being invited in rather than closed out by stacks of look-alike buildings. We think of it as being able to relate to a place, as having a connection with it, feeling like we belong there.

This sense of soul has a weathered quality. You can read life into it, as you can into a worn leather sofa that's been beaten up in repeated moves from one house to another, clambered over by two or three generations of kids, used as a scratching post by long-forgotten cats. It doesn't demand that you be on your best behavior or dress appropriately; you can relax into it. It goes beyond formal or informal, like the paintings admired by the protagonist of Teju Cole's novel *Open City* when he visits New York's Museum of American Folk Art. "The artists lacked formal training, but their work had soul," he reflects. And that's part of the beauty of it: the usual measures of achievement do not apply. Someone with little or no schooling may have soul, while another with multiple advanced degrees may seem lacking in it. A woman who has never set foot beyond her mountain village may have soul, as may a quadriplegic unable to set foot anywhere at all, while the most traveled, most physically daring adventurer may seem oddly soulless.

Americans are probably most familiar with this in terms of soul music, which often voices deep pain yet by a certain alchemy transforms pain into beauty, the bitter into the hauntingly bittersweet. It celebrates the harshly imperfect, speaking of experience, even of survival, and turning the harshness of life into gratefulness for it. But perhaps all great music, no matter the genre, is soul music. It's music that moves you, sometimes literally, which is why I sometimes find myself dancing to a Beethoven symphony or to the ecstatic chanting of Nusrat Fateh Ali Khan, at least when there's nobody else around. Music is not only an expression of soul but a carrier of it, which is why it's so often banned by fundamentalist regimes. Soul never sits well with dogma.

Just as there's an undeniable presence to soul, there's an equally undeniable sense of absence when it's missing, whether in a place or in a person. Even someone who's never heard the adage that the eyes are the windows of the soul will shrink from the adamant conviction in the eyes of a fanatic holding a knife to someone's throat, or from the panicked blankness of post-traumatic stress disorder or the dispirited listlessness of those worn down by chronic poverty or constant abuse. It's as though something deeply human has been taken away. Look into such eyes, and it seems like there's nobody at home. You might even think that it really is possible to steal someone's soul.

But here is the problem with thinking in terms of soulfulness or soullessness: soul is not a matter of either/or, of presence or absence. While "a" soul might possibly be owned or stolen, or even sold as in a Faustian pact, the quality that is soul cannot. I find myself searching for a different language, then—for other ways of thinking about soul that might come closer to the essence of it—only to end up in the humbling position of a writer at a loss for words, trying to define the undefinable. But since I am what you might call a stubborn soul, let me attempt one more approach in the language we do have, and ask what we mean when we talk (to the extent we still do) of brave souls and timid ones.

Soul as a matter of courage? If so, it's not the obvious courage of a lauded hero, but the quieter, everyday kind of courage it takes to be open to the world. It's not that some people have no soul, but that the quality of soul in them seems to have shriveled, turned in on itself as though in retreat. They have taken a defensive position, and built a wall around themselves.

Walls are built out of fear, out of the desire to keep the world at bay. When cities were still walled, what was beyond the walls was seen as dangerous; unknown and unpredictable, it was thought of as wilderness. Safer by far to stay closed in. At night the citizens literally retreated, shutting the gates until dawn. And while there appeared to be security in this, there was also isolation, and an underlying sense of radical insecurity. To live within fortified walls was to be constantly on the alert for possible attack; what was meant to make you feel safe also made you more conscious of how unsafe you might be.

Walls, that is, have a dual effect. "Before I built a wall I'd ask to know / What I was walling in or walling out," wrote Robert Frost in his poem "Mending Wall." That's an excellent question, because what is true of stone and concrete walls is also true of mental ones. You wall yourself off when you expect the worst. Better the devil you know, you tell yourself, than the unpredictability of the unknown; better to be ruled by the past than by hope for a different future. You try to persuade yourself you are strong because you have made yourself impregnable, but you live nonetheless in a state of fear. Your view is blocked. You have closed the gates and walled yourself off from the world—even, at the extreme, against the world.

And if the gates remain open? Could having soul be a matter of being brave enough to be vulnerable—to acknowledge the risks of being vulnerable, that is, and to willingly embrace them nonetheless? Because risks they are. Those I think of as brave souls know this. In a way, they're the personification of soul music: they often bear the scars of bitter experience, and yet are not ruled by fear or resentment. Not that they are saints; they are as deeply flawed as you or I, but they accept their own flaws, and thus those of others. And if they seem to have gained a certain ease with the world, it is a hard-earned one. It's as though they have persevered and come out the other end of hardship worn and weathered, but with a deeper appreciation of what it is to be alive. They welcome both the unknown and the unknowable, explore without preconceptions, and place their faith in trust, preferring the chance of being proved wrong to the illusory certainty of always being right.

Open and closed: perhaps these are the terms in which we need to think. Not soulful or soulless, nor brave souls or timid ones, but open-souled and closed-souled. Where the latter contracts and retreats from others, the former expands, reaches out, is open to the world instead of guarded against it.

Few people are entirely one way or the other, of course. Most of us can open up on occasion, yet are still tempted to close ourselves off when under stress. We struggle with trust, and uncertainty, and doubt, and find ourselves searching for the security of conviction even as we recognize its falseness. We're brave at times, fearful at others; we're contradictory, and paradoxical, and fallible. Which is to say, we're human. But at our best, we respond to soul with soul, as happened when someone whose real name I don't even know posted a comment on an early attempt of mine to puzzle out what we mean when we say that someone has soul.

"I'm not sure I understand," she wrote (a gentle way of saying that I hadn't been very clear), "but I think I recognize it. It's what makes my heart swell—what makes me glad to be alive." And then: "Is this it?"

ACKNOWLEDGMENTS

I cannot possibly do justice here to the number of people who have helped refine my thinking (to the extent that it has been refined) over the years, both in conversation and in books. But I do want to express special gratitude to the readers of *accidentaltheologist.com*, who refused to rest easy with my capsule description of the site as "an agnostic eye on religion, politics, and existence" and pressed me for more. This book is the more.

Deep thanks to Rebecca Brown, David Guterson, and Pico Iyer, superb writers and thinkers who were both generous and tough-minded as they read early versions of the manuscript; to Chris Anderson and Bruno Giussani of TED for giving me an extraordinary platform from which to begin my exploration of the vital role of doubt; and to good friends in Seattle, New York, London, and Jerusalem for their unstinting support and encouragement.

I have had the privilege and the great good fortune to work from the inception of this book with Riverhead Books editorial director Rebecca Saletan, whose judgment I value beyond words. Huge thanks also to the whole Riverhead team, including Katie Freeman, Anna Jardine, Sabila Khan, Geoff Kloske, Michelle Koufopoulos, and Jynne Dilling Martin, all of whom have gone above and beyond in their support.

And as ever, immense gratitude to my friend and agent Gloria Loomis, the constant in my writing life, who has always had faith in me. Thank you.

SOURCES

Note: Since a full bibliography would run far too long, I have listed only books, authors, and other resources either referred to or directly quoted in this book.

Auden, W. H. "Friday's Child," in *Collected Poems*. Vintage, 1991.

Augustine. *Confessions*. Oxford University Press, 2009.

Becker, Ernest. *The Birth and Death of Meaning*. Free Press, 1971.

———. *The Denial of Death*. Free Press, 1997.

Benjamin, Walter. *Reflections*. Schocken, 1986.

Berger, Peter L. *The Sacred Canopy: Elements of a Sociological Theory of Religion*. Anchor, 1990.

Blake, William. "Songs of Innocence," in *Complete Poems*. Penguin, 1978.

Burkert, Walter. *The Creation of the Sacred: Tracks of Biology in Early Religion*. Harvard University Press, 1998.

Camus, Albert. *The Myth of Sisyphus*. Vintage, 1991.

Cole, Teju. *Open City*. Random House, 2011.

Coleridge, Samuel Taylor. *Biographia Literaria*. Princeton University Press, 1985.

Dawkins, Richard. *The God Delusion*. Houghton Mifflin, 2006.

Dennett, Daniel. *Breaking the Spell: Religion as a Natural Phenomenon*. Viking, 2006.

Dickinson, Emily. "I Dwell in Possibility," in *Complete Poems*. Back Bay Books, 1976.

Dyson, Freeman. "The Two Windows," in *How Large Is God? Voices of Scientists and Theologians*, edited by John Marks Templeton. Templeton Foundation Press, 1997.

Einstein, Albert. *Ideas and Opinions*. Broadway Books, 1995.

———. In Max Jammer, *Einstein and Religion: Physics and Theology*. Princeton University Press, 2002.

Eliot, T. S. "East Coker" in *Four Quartets*. Mariner Books, 1968.

Erigena, John Scotus. In Deirdre Carabine, *John Scottus Eriugena*. Oxford University Press, 2000.

Feynman, Richard P. *The Pleasure of Finding Things Out*. Perseus, 1999.

Firestein, Stuart. *Ignorance: How It Drives Science*. Oxford University Press, 2012.

Freud, Sigmund. *Civilization and Its Discontents*. W. W. Norton, 2010.

———. *The Future of an Illusion*. W. W. Norton, 1989.

Frost, Robert. "Mending Wall," in *Collected Poems*. Library of America, 1995.

Gawande, Atul. *Being Mortal*. Metropolitan Books, 2014.

Gee, Henry. *The Accidental Species: Misunderstandings of Human Evolution*. University of Chicago Press, 2013.

Geertz, Clifford. *The Interpretation of Cultures*. Basic Books, 1973.

Goldstein, Rebecca. *Betraying Spinoza*. Schocken, 2009.

————. *Plato at the Googleplex*. Pantheon, 2014.

————. *36 Arguments for the Existence of God*. Pantheon, 2010.

Graham, Ronald. In *To Infinity and Beyond*. BBC Horizon, 2010. https://www.youtube.com/watch?v=UPrT2IoNtio.

Greene, Graham. *The Heart of the Matter*. Penguin, 2004.

————. *The Power and the Glory*. Penguin, 2003.

————. *The Quiet American*. Penguin, 2004.

Guillaume, Alfred. *The Life of Muhammad: A Translation of Ishaq's Sirat Rasul Allah*. Oxford University Press, 1955.

Harris, Sam. *The End of Faith: Religion, Terror, and the Future of Reason*. W. W. Norton, 2004.

Hilbert, David. In David Foster Wallace, *Everything and More*. W. W. Norton, 2003.

Hitchens, Christopher. *God Is Not Great: How Religion Poisons Everything*. Twelve Books, 2006.

Huxley, Aldous. *Brave New World*. Harper Perennial, 2006.

————. *The Doors of Perception*. Harper Perennial, 2008.

James, Henry. *The Turn of the Screw*. Bantam Classics, 1981.

James, William. *Pragmatism*. Penguin, 2000.

————. *The Varieties of Religious Experience: A Study in Human Nature*. Penguin, 1982.

————. *The Will to Believe and Other Essays in Popular Philosophy*. Dover, 1960.

Jonas, Hans. *Mortality and Morality*. Northwestern University Press, 1986.

Judt, Tony. *When the Facts Change*. Penguin, 2015.

Kafka, Franz. *Parables and Paradoxes*. Schocken, 1961.

Keats, John. In Ou Li, *Keats and Negative Capability*. Bloomsbury, 2011.

Kierkegaard, Søren. "Concluding Unscientific Postscript," in
The Essential Kierkegaard, edited by Howard V. Hong and
Edna H. Hong. Princeton University Press, 2000.

Kuhn, Thomas. *The Structure of Scientific Revolutions.*
University of Chicago Press, 1962.

La Haye, Tim, and Jerry B. Jenkins. *The Rapture.* Tyndale
House, 2007.

Lakoff, George, and Mark Johnson. *Metaphors We Live By.*
University of Chicago Press, 2003.

Larkin, Philip. "Aubade," in *Complete Poems.* Farrar, Straus
and Giroux, 2013.

Lightman, Alan. *The Accidental Universe.* Vintage, 2014.

Maimonides. *A Maimonides Reader*, edited by Isadore Twersky.
Behrman House, 1972.

Maslow, Abraham. *Religions, Values, and Peak Experiences.*
Penguin, 1994.

Matthiessen, Peter. *At Play in the Fields of the Lord.* Vintage, 1991.

Montesquieu. *Persian Letters.* Penguin, 1973.

Muir, John. *My First Summer in the Sierra.* Dover, 2004.

Nagel, Thomas. *Mind and Cosmos.* Oxford University Press,
2012.

———. *Mortal Questions.* Cambridge University Press, 2012.

———. *Secular Philosophy and the Religious Temperament.*
Oxford University Press, 2009.

———. *The View From Nowhere.* Oxford University Press, 1986.

———. "What Is It Like to Be a Bat?" in *Mortal Questions.*

Nietzsche, Friedrich. *Thus Spake Zarathustra.* Cambridge
University Press, 2006.

Otto, Rudolf. *The Idea of the Holy.* Oxford University Press, 1958.

Padilla, Tony. In "Astounding: $1+2+3+4+5+ \ldots = -\frac{1}{12}$."
Numberphile, 2014. https://www.youtube.com/
watch?v=w-I6XTVZXww.

Pascal, Blaise. *Pensées*. Penguin, 1995.

Pew Forum on Religion and Public Life. "Religious Landscape
Study." http://www.pewforum.org/religious
-landscape-study.

Rumi, Jalal ad-Din. *The Essential Rumi*, translated by Coleman
Barks. HarperOne, 2004.

———. *The Soul of Rumi*, translated by Coleman Barks.
HarperOne, 2002.

Ruskin, John. *Selected Writings*. Oxford University Press, 2009.

Sacks, Oliver. "My Own Life," in *The New York Times*, February
19, 2015.

Sartre, Jean-Paul. *Being and Nothingness*. Washington Square
Press, 1993.

Scheffler, Samuel, and Niko Kolodny. *Death and the Afterlife*.
Oxford University Press, 2013.

Scholem, Gershom. *Sabbetai Zevi*. Princeton University Press,
1976.

Schopenhauer, Arthur. *Essays and Aphorisms*. Penguin, 1973.

Shanley, John Patrick. *Doubt: A Parable*. Theatre
Communications Group, 2005.

Shelley, Mary. *Frankenstein*. Penguin Classics, 2013.

Solnit, Rebecca. *A Field Guide to Getting Lost*. Viking Penguin,
2005.

Spinoza, Benedict de. *A Spinoza Reader: The Ethics and Other
Works*, edited and translated by Edwin Curley. Princeton
University Press, 1994.

Tegmark, Max. *Our Mathematical Universe*. Vintage, 2015.

Thiel, Peter. In "When I'm Sixty-Four," by Roger Cohen in *The New York Times*, December 24, 2013.

Twain, Mark. *Autobiographical Writings*, edited by R. Kent Rasmussen. Penguin, 2012.

Voltaire. "Letters," in *The Portable Voltaire*, edited by Ben Ray Redman. Penguin, 1980.

Wallace, David Foster. *Everything and More*. W. W. Norton, 2003.

Warren, Rick. *The Purpose Driven Life*. Zondervan, 2002.

Weisman, Alan. *The World Without Us*. St. Martin's, 2007.

Woolf, Virginia. *Moments of Being*, edited by Jeanne Schulkind. Mariner Books, 1985.

Yeats, William Butler. "The Second Coming," in *The Collected Poems and Four Plays*, edited by M. L. Rosenthal. Scribner, 1996.

Zilboorg, Gregory. *Psychoanalysis and Religion*. Farrar, Straus and Cudahy, 1962.